Asthma

Diseases and Disorders

ReferencePoint
Press®

San Diego, CA

Select* books in the Compact Research series include:

Current Issues

Abortion
Animal Experimentation
Cloning
Conflict in the Middle East
The Death Penalty
DNA Evidence and
    Investigation
Drugs and Sports
Energy Alternatives
Genetic Engineering
Global Warming and
    Climate Change

Gun Control
Immigration
Islam
National Security
Nuclear Weapons and
    Security
Obesity
Stem Cells
Teen Smoking
Terrorist Attacks
Video Games
World Energy Crisis

Diseases and Disorders

ADHD
Alzheimer's Disease
Anorexia
Autism
Bipolar Disorders
Epilepsy

HPV
Phobias
Post-Traumatic Stress
    Disorder
Sexually Transmitted
    Diseases

Drugs

Antidepressants
Club Drugs
Cocaine and Crack
Hallucinogens
Heroin
Inhalants
Marijuana

Methamphetamine
Nicotine and Tobacco
Painkillers
Performance-Enhancing
    Drugs
Prescription Drugs
Steroids

Energy and the Environment

Biofuels
Deforestation
Hydrogen Power

Solar Power
Wind Power

*For a complete list of titles please visit www.referencepointpress.com.

COMPACT *Research*

Asthma

Hal Marcovitz

Diseases and Disorders

ReferencePoint
Press®

San Diego, CA

© 2010 ReferencePoint Press, Inc.

For more information, contact:
ReferencePoint Press, Inc.
PO Box 27779
San Diego, CA 92198
www.ReferencePointPress.com

Picture credits:
Cover: iStockphoto.com
Maury Aaseng: 33–35, 47–49, 62–64, 77–79
AP Images: 17
Science Photo Library: 15

LIBRARY OF CONGRESS CATALOGING-IN-PUBLICATION DATA

Marcovitz, Hal.
  Asthma / by Hal Marcovitz.
    p. cm. — (Compact research series)
  Includes bibliographical references and index.
  ISBN-13: 978-1-60152-104-0 (hardback)
  ISBN-10: 1-60152-104-9 (hardback)
  1. Asthma—Juvenile literature. I. Title.
  RC591.M37   2010
  616.2'38—dc22
                                             2009036844

Contents

Foreword

"Where is the knowledge we have lost in information?"

—T.S. Eliot, "The Rock."

As modern civilization continues to evolve, its ability to create, store, distribute, and access information expands exponentially. The explosion of information from all media continues to increase at a phenomenal rate. By 2020 some experts predict the worldwide information base will double every 73 days. While access to diverse sources of information and perspectives is paramount to any democratic society, information alone cannot help people gain knowledge and understanding. Information must be organized and presented clearly and succinctly in order to be understood. The challenge in the digital age becomes not the creation of information, but how best to sort, organize, enhance, and present information.

ReferencePoint Press developed the *Compact Research* series with this challenge of the information age in mind. More than any other subject area today, researching current issues can yield vast, diverse, and unqualified information that can be intimidating and overwhelming for even the most advanced and motivated researcher. The *Compact Research* series offers a compact, relevant, intelligent, and conveniently organized collection of information covering a variety of current topics ranging from illegal immigration and deforestation to diseases such as anorexia and meningitis.

The series focuses on three types of information: objective single-author narratives, opinion-based primary source quotations, and facts and statistics. The clearly written objective narratives provide context and reliable background information. Primary source quotes are carefully selected and cited, exposing the reader to differing points of view. And facts and statistics sections aid the reader in evaluating perspectives. Presenting these key types of information creates a richer, more balanced learning experience.

For better understanding and convenience, the series enhances information by organizing it into narrower topics and adding design features that make it easy for a reader to identify desired content. For example, in *Compact Research: Illegal Immigration*, a chapter covering the economic impact of illegal immigration has an objective narrative explaining the various ways the economy is impacted, a balanced section of numerous primary source quotes on the topic, followed by facts and full-color illustrations to encourage evaluation of contrasting perspectives.

The ancient Roman philosopher Lucius Annaeus Seneca wrote, "It is quality rather than quantity that matters." More than just a collection of content, the *Compact Research* series is simply committed to creating, finding, organizing, and presenting the most relevant and appropriate amount of information on a current topic in a user-friendly style that invites, intrigues, and fosters understanding.

Asthma at a Glance

What Is Asthma?

Asthma is a condition in which the bronchial passages in the lungs become constricted, inflamed, and coated with mucus, cutting down on the patient's ability to breathe.

Asthma Affects Children and Adults

There are many varieties of asthma, the most common of which is child-onset asthma, which afflicts children. Adults can also contract asthma; their symptoms are often prompted by exercising, coughing, or the environment in which they work.

Who Suffers from Asthma?

Some 22 million Americans have been diagnosed with asthma, 9.5 million of whom are under the age of 18.

Asthma Triggers

Allergens such as pollen, pet dander, and the fecal matter from dust mites and cockroaches are common triggers. Asthma symptoms can also be triggered by cigarette smoke, chemicals found in household products, and air pollution.

Identifying Asthma

Patients take spirometry tests, which gauge the strength of their lungs. Doctors look for triggers by testing for allergies using skin prick, intradermal, skin patch, and blood tests.

Severe Consequences

Struggling to breathe, asthma patients can lapse into respiratory distress. About 200,000 asthma patients a year are treated in hospital emergency rooms. About 4,000 patients a year die during asthma attacks.

Athletes and Asthma

Despite their breathing problems, many asthma patients have gone on to athletic careers, including football star Jerome Bettis, Olympic swimmers Tom Dolan and Amy Van Dyken, and track star Jackie Joyner-Kersee.

Standard Treatments

The two main drugs employed to treat asthma patients are corticosteroids, which reduce the inflammation in bronchial tubes, and bronchodilators, which relax the bronchial tube muscles.

Alternative Treatments

Asthma patients have had varying levels of success with alternative treatments such as herbal remedies, yoga, acupuncture, and breathing techniques.

Overview

❝I was a sickly, delicate boy, suffered much from asthma, and frequently had to be taken away on trips to find a place where I could breathe.❞

—Theodore Roosevelt, twenty-sixth president of the United States.

What Is Asthma?

Asthma is a condition in which the airways in the lungs, known as bronchial tubes, become inflamed and constricted. Asthma is often triggered by a reaction to allergens, such as pollen or pet dander, or by other substances in the air, including cigarette smoke and pollutants. Asthma patients often struggle to breathe. Other physical reactions to asthma include coughing and wheezing, which is a high-pitched whistling sound made by patients as they breathe.

Asthma is not a communicable disease, meaning a healthy person cannot contract it through personal contact with an asthma sufferer, as he or she would contract a cold or flu. Patients develop asthma on their own, often in childhood, although it is not unusual for people to become asthmatic as they grow older. Indeed, some patients do not develop asthmatic conditions until they are in their 70s. "Asthma is not, in the commonly recognized sense, a specific disease," says Phil Lieberman, a professor of medicine and pediatrics at the University of Tennessee College of Medicine. "Rather, it is a 'condition,' an incompletely understood abnormality, and its exact cause is unknown. In fact, there are probably multiple causes."[1]

During an asthma attack the muscles of the bronchial walls tighten while extra mucus builds up to block the airways. This condition causes the bronchial tubes to narrow and results in symptoms that can be as minor as wheezing and as severe as a fatal asthma attack in which the patient is unable to draw breaths. Says Lieberman, "In many, the condition is extremely mild and does not significantly interfere with quality of life. In other cases, the illness can be debilitating."[2]

Symptoms Surface in Childhood

Most asthma patients first manifest symptoms by the age of five. In fact, asthma is regarded as the most common chronic illness among children, with more than 9.5 million young people in America suffering from the condition. One of those young asthma patients is Malia Obama, the daughter of President Barack Obama and First Lady Michelle Obama. "She was only three when she came into the kitchen and said, 'Daddy, I'm having trouble breathing,' which is the worst thing you want to hear from your kids,"[3] the president recalled. Unsure of what was wrong with Malia, the Obamas took their daughter to a hospital, where she was admitted for observation overnight.

Doctors suspect there may be many reasons asthma strikes first in childhood. Young children receive many vaccinations as well as antibiotics to treat infections, and it is possible that the drugs have an effect on the ability of the lungs to endure dust, pollutants, and allergens.

A change in the lifestyles of children over the past few decades may have also contributed to the trend. Today's children spend less time outdoors than young people of the past, instead watching TV and playing video games. Moreover, homes are much more energy efficient now than they were years ago, meaning less fresh air circulates indoors. With homes sealed tight against the weather, dust, pet dander, and other airborne particles tend to stay inside, where they are breathed in by children.

> " **Asthma is not a communicable disease, meaning a healthy person cannot contract it through personal contact with an asthma sufferer, as he or she would contract a cold or flu.** "

Many Varieties of Asthma

Although all asthma patients share similar symptoms, there are several varieties of the condition. Each is prompted by different factors.

Child-onset asthma is a condition that first surfaces in childhood. About half the patients develop symptoms by the age of two while most others manifest symptoms by the age of five. When children are young their lungs are very sensitive to allergens, pollutants, and other environmental factors. Also, doctors believe child-onset asthma may be genetic, meaning children inherit allergic conditions from their parents or other relatives that can develop into asthma.

Adult-onset asthma strikes people over the age of 20. Half the cases of adult-onset asthma are linked to allergies that do not show up until people enter their adult years. The other half may be due to particles in the environment that the patients may encounter in their adult years. As adults, they may develop symptoms after moving to a new city where certain types of pollutants are more prevalent than they were in the patients' former hometowns.

> "Young children receive many vaccinations as well as antibiotics to treat infections, and it is possible that the drugs have an effect on the ability of the lungs to endure dust, pollutants, and allergens."

Exercise-induced asthma manifests itself during exercise. People who cough or wheeze after running or playing basketball or performing similar activities may have asthma that is prompted by physical exertion.

In cough-induced asthma, the main symptom is a cough, rather than wheezing or shortness of breath. Cough-induced asthma is difficult to diagnose because doctors often mistake it for hay fever, bronchitis, or similar maladies of the bronchial passages.

Nocturnal asthma occurs only at night, usually between midnight and 8:00 A.M. Many patients wake up at 2:00 or 3:00 A.M., finding themselves wheezing and short of breath. Nocturnal asthma occurs as the body rests. During times of rest, levels of adrenaline and cortisol in the blood are low. These two chemicals help the body react to stress—one of their jobs is to help the lungs function during stressful periods. Therefore, when the patient is asleep and levels of adrenaline and cortisol are low, the lungs are often unable to handle the stresses of allergens and other particles in the air. As the patient wakes up and levels of adrenaline and cortisol return to normal, the patient's symptoms often go away.

Occupational asthma is triggered by environmental conditions in the workplace, such as a factory where chemical vapors or particles float in the air. People who work outdoors may come in contact with a lot of pollen, dust, or mold. Even office workers may find themselves suffering from occupational asthma if they cannot tolerate the fibers in the carpets under their desks.

> **Even office workers may find themselves suffering from occupational asthma if they cannot tolerate the fibers in the carpets under their desks.**

Steroid-resistant asthma is a condition in which patients do not respond to medication that contains steroids. Steroids are well-known because of their abuse by athletes who inject them to build up muscle mass, but steroids also contain anti-inflammatory properties, which is why doctors often prescribe them for asthma patients. If a patient's asthma proves to be resistant to steroids, doctors will look for other anti-inflammatory drugs to control the patient's symptoms.

Managing Asthma

Asthma is not a curable condition. Drugs as well as other therapies help patients manage their symptoms, but there are no treatments that can make the condition go away. However, many asthma patients find that their symptoms disappear on their own as they grow older.

Patients whose symptoms persist must rely on a variety of therapies to manage their condition, including finding the medications and dosages that work best for them and learning what substances may trigger allergic reactions. Most asthma patients learn how to manage their symptoms, but some occasionally suffer asthma attacks—conditions in which their bronchial passages narrow, making breathing difficult.

During asthma attacks, patients may find themselves short of breath, and they may cough or wheeze. They may feel a tightness in their chests. They may find it difficult to speak because of their wheezing or because they are unable to catch their breath. Most asthma patients use two types of medications—one for daily therapy to keep their lungs open and a stronger drug to be used in the event of an asthma attack. Most asthma drugs are consumed in mist form through a device known as an inhaler.

Young Boys More at Risk than Girls

According to the Centers for Disease Control and Prevention, 15 percent of boys and 11 percent of girls under the age of 18 are asthma patients; doctors believe this trend is because young girls have larger bronchial passages than young boys. As adolescents and adults, though, the trend reverses. As they grow older, female asthma patients outnumber male asthma patients by 40 percent.

These trends were confirmed in a 2008 study by Harvard University Medical School in Massachusetts, which followed more than 1,000 young asthma patients over a period of eight years as they grew into adults. The authors of the study suggest that hormonal changes in adolescent girls may help make them more vulnerable to allergens. "Hormones can play a key role in influencing asthma symptoms and severity, suggesting that gender is an important factor in asthma,"[4] says Leanne Male, a spokesperson for Asthma UK, an asthma patients' support group in Great Britain.

> The bronchial passages in adult women are naturally thinner than those found in adult men, which means many women may have a lower tolerance for the conditions that prompt asthma attacks.

In addition, the authors of the Harvard study believe that the bronchial passages in adult women are naturally thinner than those found in adult men, which means many women may have a lower tolerance for the conditions that prompt asthma attacks. "The differences in gender begin at the time of transition into early puberty,"[5] says Kelan G. Tantisiria, the Harvard physician who headed the study.

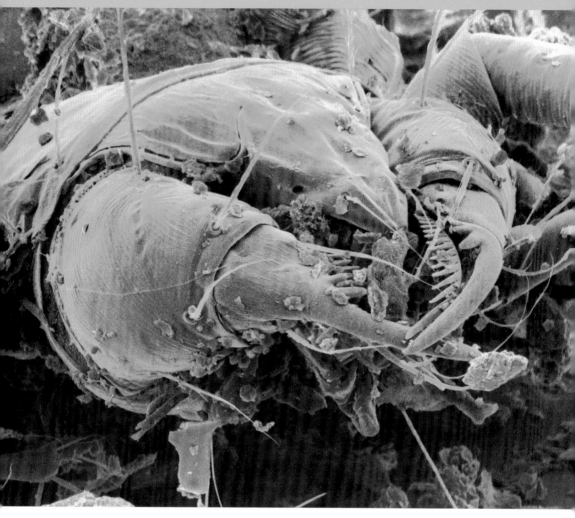

A dust mite forages among skin scales found in a sample of household dust in this magnified color-enhanced scanning electron micrograph. Dust mite droppings are one of the many allergens that can trigger asthma attacks.

What Causes Asthma?

Asthma is prevalent throughout American society: Some 22 million Americans—about 7 percent of the population—have been diagnosed with the condition. In recent years physicians have come to believe that asthma is caused by a variety of factors, including a family history of asthma and exposure to an environment where allergens, dust, and pollutants are common. Another possible cause is an immune system that responds to allergens and pollutants by causing inflammation and a shrinking of the bronchial passages as well as the production of the mucus that coats the walls of the passages, further constricting the airways.

Many people have allergies and are able to tolerate them well. Some people suffer from hay fever, which is caused by an allergy to pollen that drifts through the air. Usually, their symptoms are confined to occasional sneezing and watery eyes, and they can often find relief in over-the-counter allergy medications. Asthma patients have much more severe reactions to their allergies—they may wheeze, cough, or lapse into respiratory distress as they gasp for air.

> " Asthma is prevalent throughout American society: Some 22 million Americans— about 7 percent of the population— have been diagnosed with the condition. "

Allergies are not the only triggers. Bronchitis is an infection caused by a virus that affects the bronchial tubes. In a person who does not have asthma, the virus may trigger a persistent cough for a few days, but in an asthma patient bronchitis could trigger an attack. The droppings from dust mites, which are microscopic creatures that live on human skin dander, often prompt allergic attacks in asthma patients. Household products such as paints, furniture stains, cleaners, and similar chemicals could cause an asthmatic reaction. Brian Thomas, a 41-year-old New Yorker, thought he had his asthma under control, but when his roommates painted the apartment, Thomas suffered an asthma attack. "My chest felt tight and burned, and I just couldn't catch my breath," he recalled. Thomas's landlord came to his rescue by hailing a taxicab to take him to a nearby hospital emergency room. Later, Thomas said, "I thought I would die right there [in the cab]."[6]

Air Quality Index

Each day meteorologists providing weather reports on TV and in other media report the Air Quality Index, which has been established by the Environmental Protection Agency. This information is provided for the benefit of people with respiratory illnesses, particularly asthma.

The index is reported in numerical and color codes. An Air Quality

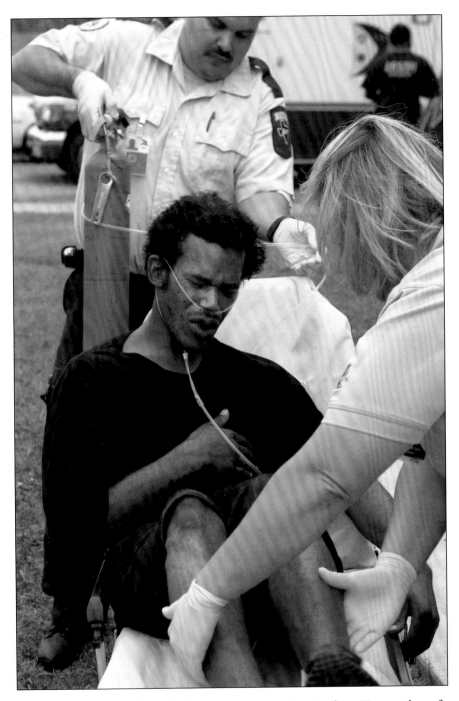

Paramedics come to the aid of a young man in Port Arthur, Texas, who suffered an asthma attack. Serious pollution problems contribute to high rates of asthma in this region.

Index of 0 to 50 is coded green, which means the air quality is good; 51 to 100 (yellow) is moderate; 101 to 150 (orange) is unhealthy for sensitive people; 151 to 200 (red) is unhealthy; 201 to 300 (purple) is very unhealthy, and 301 to 500 (maroon) is hazardous.

The Air Quality Index measures a number of substances, such as sulfur dioxide, which is emitted when oil and coal are burned, and nitrogen oxide, which is emitted through automobile tailpipes and power plants. The index also reports on the amount of particulate matter in the air, which includes dust, soot, ash, and other solid particles. The index also measures ozone, which is a toxic compound created when car exhaust mixes with oxygen and sunlight. Ground-level ozone is a particular problem for asthma patients who live in big cities where there is a lot of vehicular traffic. According to the American Lung Association, 136 million people live in areas where ozone levels are unhealthy.

How Is Asthma Treated?

Asthma was first recognized by ancient physicians about 2,500 years ago, but for centuries asthma patients suffered through their illnesses because doctors did not understand the condition, nor could they recommend effective methods of treating it. Indeed, the use of anti-inflammatory drugs to treat the condition did not find widespread use until the 1960s.

The word *asthma* is derived from the Greek word *aazein*, which means "to pant." The Greek poet Homer, who is believed to have lived in the eighth century B.C., wrote about asthma in his epic poem the *Iliad*, which told the story of the Trojan War: "Now Aphrodite, Zeus's daughter, taking Ares' hand, began to help him away, as he wheezed hard and fought to get his breath."[7]

Hippocrates, the Greek physician who lived in the fourth century B.C., accurately described the symptoms of asthma. Galen, a Greek physician who lived about 400 years later, believed the condition was caused by a blockage in the bronchial tubes but offered little relief for his patients—he recommended they drink wine laced with owl's blood. Meanwhile, physicians in ancient Egypt also diagnosed the condition, but they, too, were at a loss as to how to treat it. Archaeologists have uncovered Egyptian hieroglyphics that offer some 700 cures for asthma, including inhaling the vapors from herbs heated over bricks.

In the sixteenth century the Belgian physician Jan Baptista van

Helmont first deduced that asthma is a disease of the lungs, and in the seventeenth century the Italian physician Bernardino Ramazzini linked asthma to dust. In 1864 a British doctor, Hyde Salter, discovered that animal dander could trigger asthma.

In the early 1900s asthma medicine took a step backward as doctors accepted the notion that asthma was psychosomatic—in other words, they believed the condition was due to mental illness. Doctors believed a child's wheeze was, in fact, a cry for a mother's love. As such, asthmatic children were treated for depression. By the 1960s this notion had been dropped as medical science proved asthma was due to an inflammation of the bronchial tubes and that it should be treated with anti-inflammatory drugs.

Avoiding Allergens

Until the discovery of anti-inflammatory drugs, the doctor who may have provided the best advice to his patients was probably Moses Maimonides, a twelfth-century physician in the court of the Middle Eastern emperor Saladin. Maimonides was the first to notice that asthma symptoms grow worse during the rainy season—probably due to mold spores that accompany damp conditions. And so he urged his asthma patients to seek refuge in the desert.

In effect, Maimonides had counseled his patients to stay away from the substances that were making them cough and wheeze. Today physicians give similar advice and often urge their patients to find out what may be triggering their asthma and then take steps to avoid the triggers.

> " **Jackie Joyner-Kersee was well into her career as a track competitor when she was diagnosed with asthma at the age of 18.** "

Through a series of medical tests, patients can learn which substances may spark allergic reactions. The most common test is a skin test. A doctor will expose the patient to a small amount of an allergen through a prick, scratch, or injection. After several minutes, the test should provide a reaction such as a rash or hives.

A version of this test involves the introduction of the allergen through a patch that is placed over the skin for one to three days.

How Do People Live with Asthma?

Asthma patients learn soon after their diagnoses that they cannot take a pill to make it go away. For most patients asthma will remain a part of their lives for the rest of their lives. Francis V. Adams, an assistant professor of clinical medicine at New York University, encourages patients to become directly involved in their own therapies, learning what triggers their asthma attacks, which allergens or environmental conditions to avoid, and how to recognize their symptoms so they can be prepared if asthma attacks strike.

Adams says, "If you have asthma, it is vital first to acknowledge that you have a problem and then to deal with it by working with your physician. Too often, denying the problem only leads to unnecessary illness."[8] He says that even patients who seem to have their symptoms under control must continually be wary. Adams says he counsels patients never to let their guard down, always to have their inhalers close at hand, and to be vigilant about avoiding triggers, staying indoors on high ozone days, and taking other precautionary steps.

Winning Olympic Medals

There is no reason asthma patients cannot maintain full and active lives. Five American presidents—Bill Clinton, Calvin Coolidge, John Kennedy, Theodore Roosevelt, and Woodrow Wilson—have suffered from asthma. Many top American athletes have also found ways to overcome asthma and compete at a high level.

Jackie Joyner-Kersee was well into her career as a track competitor when she was diagnosed with asthma at the age of 18. Growing up in East St. Louis, Illinois, Joyner-Kersee occasionally suffered from breathing difficulties. A doctor misdiagnosed her illness as bronchitis, but when she arrived for her freshman year at the University of California–Los Angeles, she received a correct diagnosis.

At first Joyner-Kersee refused to believe she had asthma. She figured she would not have been able to compete in track events with asthma. So she ignored her doctor's orders, refused to use her inhaler, and soon found herself coughing and wheezing in the smoggy Los Angeles air. "My biggest fear was that I would have an attack in a competition, and I didn't want that to happen. And that was the only obstacle that could beat me. So I stopped looking at the doctor as an enemy and started respecting my doctor's knowledge and using him as a coach to help me,"[9] she says.

Joyner-Kersee came to terms with her asthma. She used her inhaler as prescribed and went on to a stellar career in track that included winning five Olympic medals. As Joyner-Kersee's case shows, asthma patients can never rid themselves of their conditions, but they can certainly lead normal lives. As long as they are willing to accept their diagnoses, they can control their asthma instead of letting asthma control them.

What Is Asthma?

How Do The Lungs Work?

Asthma is an incurable disorder that affects one of the body's most important organs, the lungs. A primary mission of the lungs is to supply oxygen to the blood, which circulates it throughout the body. Without oxygen, the body's other organs would shut down within minutes.

The delivery of oxygen to the rest of the body starts in the bronchial tubes. In the lungs the system of bronchial tubes resembles an upside-down branching tree with the trachea, or windpipe, serving as the trunk. Covering the bronchial tubes—the "tree branches"—are millions of tiny air sacs known as alveoli. The walls of the alveoli are lined with capillaries, which are tiny blood vessels. When air is drawn into the lungs through the physical act of breathing, the air enters the alveoli, striking the walls and entering the capillaries, where the oxygen in the air mixes with blood. The blood then carries the oxygen to the other parts of the body.

Meanwhile, another gas found in the blood—carbon dioxide—is expelled into the alveoli and then through the bronchial tubes, where it is exhaled by the body. Carbon dioxide is a waste product generated when the body metabolizes glucose, which is a common sugar found in many foods. When the lungs fail to expel carbon dioxide from the body, a condition known as hypercapnia could occur. People who suffer from hypercapnia experience headaches, confusion, increased blood pressure, convulsions, and unconsciousness. Hypercapnia can also be fatal. Therefore, the purpose of the lungs is to draw oxygen into the body and expel carbon dioxide out of the body. During an asthma attack, patients can suffer from symptoms of both oxygen loss and hypercapnia.

An Asthmatic's Lungs

In a person who has asthma, the bronchial tubes respond to pollen, pollutants, and other substances by constricting. That means they become narrow and cut down on the amount of oxygen that can enter the alveoli as well as the amount of carbon dioxide that leaves the body. The constriction of the bronchial walls occurs because the muscles in the walls cramp up or go into spasms. The narrowed bronchial tubes are what cause the asthma patient to make wheezing sounds while trying to breathe.

The bronchial walls also become inflamed, meaning they are red and swollen. Also, the lungs produce an excess of mucus that coats the walls, further restricting the airways and leaving little room for oxygen to flow into the lungs. Says Phil Lieberman from the University of Tennessee College of Medicine, "What is known as our 'work of breathing,' or the energy that must be put into each breath, increases, and the sufferer experiences shortness of breath, one of the cardinal symptoms of this condition."[10]

Moreover, Lieberman says, breathing also becomes difficult because the bronchial tubes naturally expand during inhalation. If they are unable to expand, which occurs in asthma, the patient finds air trapped in the lungs that he or she cannot expel. "Patients feel as if they are 'breathing off the top of their lungs,'" he says. "No matter how hard they attempt to breathe, the already-filled air sacs cannot be expanded further because of trapped air."[11]

The Warning Signs

Asthmatics can recognize some common warning signs as an asthma attack approaches. In many cases the warning signs start making themselves known 24 to 48 hours before an asthma attack, but it is not unusual for the warning signs to occur just a few hours before the attack. Patients may find themselves coughing frequently. They may develop a mild wheeze and shortness of breath. They may feel weary or weak, especially while exercising. Runny noses and congestion are often among the early warning signs.

> **Without oxygen the body's . . . organs would shut down within minutes.**

Sandra Fusco-Walker, a New Jersey resident whose two young daughters suffer from asthma, noticed that one of the girls would often suffer an asthma attack after visiting the girl's grandmother, who smokes. Clearly, the tobacco smoke served as a trigger for the girl's asthma. "I noticed that one of my daughters rubbed her nose when breathing became difficult,"[12] says Fusco-Walker.

There are other warning signs that are not as easy to recognize. In most cases these conditions are common reactions to allergens—such as developing a rash or itch, stomachache, headache, back pain, sore shoulders, raspy voice, constant thirst, and a flushed or pale complexion. For somebody who does not suffer from asthma, these reactions will clear up on their own after a period of a few hours or days. In asthma patients, though, these allergic reactions can progress into respiratory distress—an asthma attack.

The Asthma Attack

When the asthma attack commences, the patient's coughing and wheezing turn severe. Breathing becomes rapid but unproductive. Patients may feel pain or pressure in their chests. The muscles in the neck and chest will tighten. They may have difficulty talking and are overcome with feelings of anxiety or panic. The color may drain out of their faces, and they may start perspiring. Their lips and fingertips may turn blue.

The National Institutes of Health has established four classifications for the severity of an asthma attack. These classifications are used by doctors to assess how the patient is affected by asthma so they may prescribe the proper medications and dosages. The classifications include:

- Mild intermittent: The patient suffers an attack less than twice a week and is awakened at night by symptoms less than twice a month.

- Mild persistent: The patient suffers an asthma attack more than twice a week but less often than daily. Also, the patient is awakened by symptoms at night more than twice a month.
- Moderate persistent: The patient suffers an asthma attack daily, and the symptoms are severe enough to affect normal activities and quality of life. The patient is awakened by symptoms at night at least once a week.
- Severe persistent: The asthma attacks occur frequently and are often debilitating. The symptoms also prevent the patient from carrying out normal activities. Nighttime awakenings are frequent.

When Asthma Strikes

Asthma patients come in all shapes, sizes, and ages. During his 13-year career in the National Football League, 250-pound (113kg) running back Jerome Bettis developed a reputation as a tenacious hitter. In each game Bettis performed at a high level—despite fighting asthma throughout his career. Bettis suffered his first asthma attack on his first day of practice for his high school team in Detroit, Michigan. He recalled:

> On the first day of conditioning drills, we were supposed to run quarter-miles around the track. As I was running the first quarter-mile, I passed out. Boom! Shut down. They took me to the hospital, examined me, put me on some breathing machines, and then the doctor gave my mother the diagnosis: asthma. . . . As the doctor was telling me about asthma, I'm thinking, 'Wow, my football career is over before it even got going.[13]

Bettis was lucky—his parents knew a lot about asthma because his brother had already been diagnosed with the condition. Bettis's parents monitored his condition, kept after him to use his inhaler, and helped guide their son through his high school, college, and professional football careers.

> " When the asthma attack commences, the patient's coughing and wheezing turn severe. Breathing becomes rapid but unproductive. "

Bettis is a typical asthma patient, but so is Nathalie Carril-King, an 11-year-old New York City girl. Nathalie was 7 when she first started coughing and wheezing. Finally, her parents took her to a hospital, where she was diagnosed with asthma. "Asthma makes me scared sometimes," she says. "It can feel like someone is sitting on you. You sound like a broken-down truck, and feel weak."[14]

After four years of living with the condition, Nathalie knows the warning signs and makes sure her asthma medication is close at hand. And like Bettis, she is able to pursue an active life as a singer, dancer, and member of her school's cheerleading squad.

Complications of an Attack

Most patients can receive quick relief from asthma attacks by inhaling emergency medications to open their bronchial passages. However, complications occasionally surface. Some asthma patients endure fits of vomiting after an attack, caused by the body's desire to expel the large amounts of mucus that formed during the asthmatic episode. In severe cases the vomiting following an asthma attack may last for days as the body tries to rid itself of the excess mucus. Excessive vomiting can lead to dehydration, which may require hospitalization.

Besides trying to expel the mucus, there are other reasons asthma patients may grow sick to their stomachs and vomit after an attack. For example, as the asthma patient labors to breathe, his or her lungs expand, which pushes down on a muscle that extends below the rib cage known as the diaphragm. The diaphragm in turn exerts pressure on the stomach, which reacts by vomiting.

> " In each game Bettis performed at a high level—despite fighting asthma throughout his career. "

Also, when oxygen is cut off from the blood, many people react by feeling nauseated, which can lead to vomiting. It is similar to the nausea people feel as they ride in airplanes that do not have pressurized cockpits or visit mountaintops or other places of high altitude—in other words, places where the oxygen content of the air is less than at sea level.

Other Respiratory Diseases

The most severe cases of asthma can turn into other ailments, which fall under a category of illnesses known as chronic obstructive pulmonary disease, or COPD. Other COPD conditions include emphysema and chronic bronchitis.

Emphysema is a permanent obstruction of the alveoli. In people with emphysema, the alveoli lose their elasticity and become overinflated. Eventually, the bronchial walls deteriorate. Chronic bronchitis occurs due to the constant inflammation of the bronchial walls as well as the buildup of extra mucus on the walls. In chronic bronchitis, the bronchial walls become scarred and swollen. The mucus remains, though, obstructing the airway. Also, the bronchial tubes often lapse into spasms.

Smoking is regarded as the primary cause of emphysema and chronic bronchitis, but severe cases of asthma can also lead to COPD, which is not a reversible disease. In addition to taking drugs to keep their bronchial tubes open, COPD patients must live in homes in which the humidity is controlled, take steps to stay away from people with colds or the flu, and regularly perform exercises to keep their lungs working.

> " In severe cases the vomiting following an asthma attack may last for days as the body tries to rid itself of the excess mucus. Excessive vomiting can lead to dehydration, which may require hospitalization. "

When Asthma Can Be Fatal

Thirteen-year-old Antonio O'Bryant suffered from asthma long enough to know never to leave home without his inhaler. Still, while participating in gym class one morning, O'Bryant found himself without his inhaler when he felt an asthma attack coming on. The teacher sent for the school nurse, but when she arrived with an inhaler, O'Bryant did not have the strength to draw the mist into his lungs. An ambulance was called.

By the time O'Bryant arrived at the hospital, he had lapsed into a coma. A few days later his brain swelled from lack of oxygen. He had suffered permanent brain damage, making it unlikely he would recover from the coma. His parents then made the decision to turn off the machines that were keeping him alive. "They finally had to turn off the ventilator," his mother said later. "My baby died on Christmas day."[15]

> " Severe asthma attacks can occur at any time. Sometimes they afflict people like O'Bryant, who knew he had asthma yet had little power to stave off its most debilitating effects. "

About 4,000 people a year die during asthma attacks. Like O'Bryant, many victims experience sudden and severe symptoms. Others neglect to take their medications on time or as prescribed by their physicians. These conditions may result in acute respiratory failure in which the bronchial passages are completely closed.

Severe asthma attacks can occur at any time. Sometimes they afflict people like O'Bryant, who knew he had asthma yet had little power to stave off its most debilitating effects. Sometimes asthma afflicts people like Bettis, who never knew he suffered from the condition until he collapsed on the running track in high school. And yet Bettis's experience with asthma also shows that asthma patients can go on to lead full and active lives, although they must always be on guard for the symptoms that could leave them gasping for breath.

Primary Source Quotes*

What Is Asthma?

66 Asthma isn't very complicated: It causes a restriction of the airways. You can't breathe. It's the worst thing in the world. It's like somebody is putting a plastic bag over your head and they're choking you.99

—Jerome Bettis, *The Bus: My Life in and Out of a Helmet*. New York: Doubleday, 2007.

Bettis, an asthma patient, played running back for the St. Louis Rams and Pittsburgh Steelers in the National Football League for 13 years.

....

66 Just like my father, I was diagnosed with chronic severe asthma at a very young age. I spent a great deal of my childhood living in hospitals. My father and I struggled with daily attacks, numerous medications, constant allergies, and many uncertainties.99

—Dwight Yorke, "Living with Asthma: Our Stories," American Asthma Foundation, 2009. http://americanasthmafoundation.org.

Yorke is an engineering student at Loyola Marymount University in Los Angeles, California.

....

* Editor's Note: While the definition of a primary source can be narrowly or broadly defined, for the purposes of Compact Research, a primary source consists of: 1) results of original research presented by an organization or researcher; 2) eyewitness accounts of events, personal experience, or work experience; 3) first-person editorials offering pundits' opinions; 4) government officials presenting political plans and/or policies; 5) representatives of organizations presenting testimony or policy.

Primary Source Quotes

❝When I first learned that my older son had asthma, I imagined that it would go away in a few weeks or months. I clung to that bit of denial, I guess, because it helped ease the fear and sadness as reality sank in. Brian was only 3, and deep down my husband and I knew we were facing a serious chronic disease that would probably hang on for years, maybe even for the rest of his life.❞

—Denise Grady, "Learning to Live with Asthma," *Good Housekeeping*, August 2007.

Grady is the mother of two sons, both of whom have asthma.

❝Because COPD takes time to develop and worsen, it is usually diagnosed in middle-aged adults as symptoms become noticeable in their daily lives. While COPD typically affects people who smoke, or used to smoke, those with lung conditions such as asthma . . . are also candidates for developing the disease.❞

—Larry Johnson, "Breathing Battle: Living with COPD," *Clinton (MA) Item*, December 18, 2007.

Johnson is head of the Respiratory Care Department at Clinton Hospital in Massachusetts.

❝Active smoking plays an important role in the development (or worsening) of adult-onset asthma and progression to chronic obstructive pulmonary disease.❞

—Russell J. Hopp and Robert G. Townley, "The Origins and Characteristics of Asthma," in *Bronchial Asthma: A Guide for Practical Understanding and Treatment*, ed. M. Eric Gershwin. Totowa, NJ: Humana, 2006.

Hopp is a pediatrician at the University of Utah School of Medicine, and Townley is a pediatrician at Creighton University School of Medicine in Nebraska.

"It is recommended that patients see their physicians every one to six months, depending on the severity of their disease. Although most emergency department visits and inpatient hospitalizations resulting from asthma are preventable, these episodes commonly occur.**"**

—Centers for Disease Control and Prevention, *Health United States 2008*, March 2009. www.cdc.gov.

The Centers for Disease Control and Prevention monitors the progression of diseases in America and directs national strategies to improve the health of Americans.

"Most patients with asthma can expect to live normal lives and have a normal life expectancy. However, asthma-related deaths and disability do still occur, often because patients don't have the appropriate medication or do not take their medications properly or regularly.**"**

—Anna Murphy, *Asthma in Focus*. London: Pharmaceutical Press, 2007.

Murphy is a respiratory pharmacist at University Hospitals in Leicester, England.

"One day I was building a fence in the south Texas countryside. When I started pulling some old wooden posts out of the ground, a great deal of dust came up with those posts. After I inhaled the dust, I noticed the asthma. At first, it was only a minor annoyance. But later that night, I knew I was going to have major problems. That asthma attack lasted two days. What a nightmare.**"**

—Aaron Conor, "Dealing with Asthma: My Story," Associated Content, June 25, 2007. www.associatedcontent.com.

Conor is a graphic designer and photographer.

Facts and Illustrations

What Is Asthma?

- Worldwide about **300 million** people have been diagnosed with asthma; each year some **250,000 deaths** are attributed to asthma around the globe.

- Allergic reactions spark symptoms in about **70 percent** of asthma patients.

- About **500,000** Americans are hospitalized each year with asthma symptoms.

- **Forty-four percent** of asthma patients who are hospitalized each year are under the age of 18.

- Each day about **30,000** Americans suffer asthma attacks.

- Children between the ages of 5 and 17 miss nearly **13 million** days of school each year because of asthma. Adults with asthma miss about **10 million** days of work.

- About **40 percent** of children with asthma are born to parents who suffer from asthma.

- About **11 million** of the 22 million American asthma sufferers experience asthma attacks at least once a year.

- About **200,000** asthma patients seek help in hospital emergency rooms each year.

Inflamed Bronchial Tubes Restrict Oxygen Flow

In normal lung function, the bronchial tubes open wide to enable oxygen to enter through millions of tiny air sacs known as alveoli, which line the walls of the bronchial tubes. The oxygen then enters the blood, which carries it to the body's other organs. An asthma patient's bronchial tubes become inflamed and constricted, cutting off the supply of oxygen to the blood.

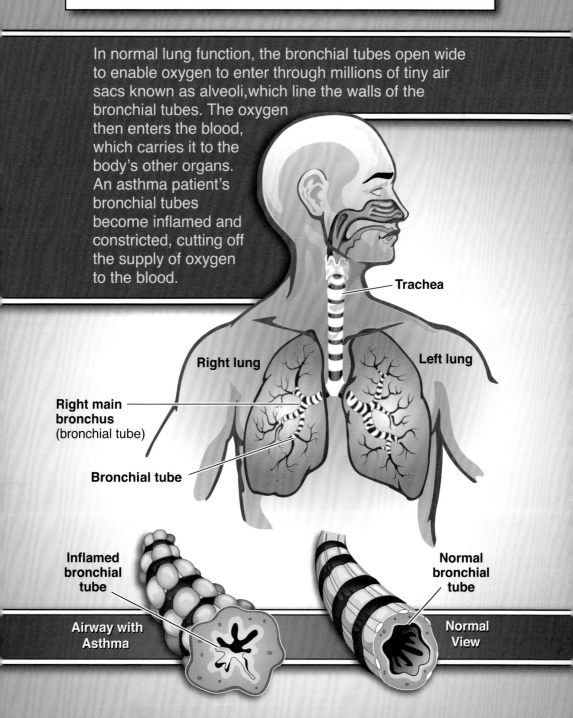

Trachea

Right lung

Left lung

Right main bronchus
(bronchial tube)

Bronchial tube

Inflamed bronchial tube

Normal bronchial tube

Airway with Asthma

Normal View

Source: *Clinical Reference Systems Pediatric Advisor*, "Asthmatic Teen Version," January 1, 2009, p.1.

Two Out of 10 Patients Experience Daily Symptoms

For many people with asthma, symptoms come and go only occasionally. But for others, symptoms are more frequent. A study by the Florida Department of Health found that 21 percent of adult asthma patients suffer daily symptoms, with 9 percent saying their symptoms are always with them while 12 percent say their symptoms come and go throughout the course of the day. In addition, 8 percent of Florida asthma patients suffer symptoms at least twice a week. Other asthma patients say they contend with their symptoms less often.

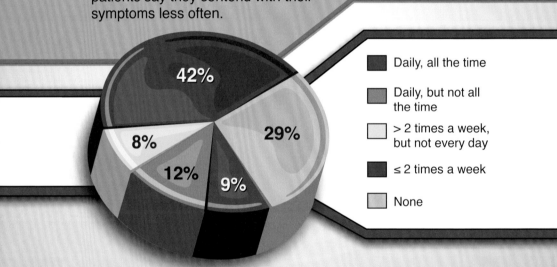

- 42%
- 29%
- 8%
- 12%
- 9%

Legend:
- Daily, all the time
- Daily, but not all the time
- > 2 times a week, but not every day
- ≤ 2 times a week
- None

Source: Florida Department of Health, *Physical Health Among Florida Adults with Current Asthma*, December 2007. www.doh.state.fl.us.

- The average length of stay for an asthma patient in the hospital is **three days**, according to the Allergy Foundation of America.

- Asthma takes the lives of about **4,000** patients each year—about 11 every day. About **65 percent** of the victims are female.

- Asthma costs the American economy about **$18 billion** a year, including about **$8 billion** in medical costs and **$10 billion** in lost productivity due to missed days at work.

Asthma by Gender, Race, and Income

Women over the age of 18 tend to suffer from asthma more than men, and women who live below the poverty line are even more likely to have asthma. Additionally, statistics from the Centers for Disease Control and Prevention show that white women are more likely to have asthma than black or Hispanic women regardless of income level and that generally white men suffer more from asthma than black or Hispanic men.

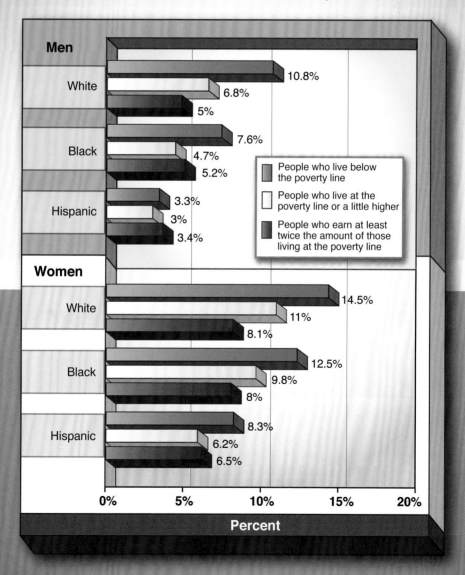

Note: According to the U.S. Department of Health and Human Services, a family of 4 lives at the poverty line if its household income is $22,050 a year or less.

Source: Centers for Disease Control and Prevention, *Health United States 2008*, March 2009. www.cdc.gov.

What Causes Asthma?

The Asthma Capitals

Each year the Asthma and Allergy Foundation of America names the top 10 "asthma capitals" of America, meaning the cities in which asthma patients suffer the most. In 2009 St. Louis, Missouri, was named the worst offender. Other cities on the list were Milwaukee, Wisconsin; Birmingham, Alabama; Chattanooga and Memphis in Tennessee; Charlotte, North Carolina; Atlanta, Georgia; Little Rock, Arkansas; and McAllen, Texas. Several of those cities have been on the list for a number of years.

In rating the cities the foundation looks at a number of factors, such as the amount of allergens and pollutants in the air, whether local authorities establish no-smoking laws for public places, the poverty rate, the number of physicians specializing in treating asthma, and similar factors. Another factor examined by the foundation is the city's death rate from asthma—in St. Louis in 2008, 2.2 asthma patients per 100,000 residents died during asthma attacks. The national average is 1.2 asthma patients per 100,000 residents.

In St. Louis, physicians said they were not surprised that their city made the list—they could tell asthma patients have a particularly hard time living in St. Louis by the number of patients they see in their practices as well as in hospital emergency rooms. "We're seeing that more patients have severe asthma that really is disabling them,"[16] said Mario Castro, a pulmonologist and professor at Washington University School of Medicine in St. Louis.

In Chattanooga, physicians said the climate and location of the Tennessee city had more to do with aggravating asthma symptoms than pollution or a lack of local antismoking laws. The city is situated in the southern part of the state, high in the Appalachian Mountains. Therefore, the air is naturally thin, and the city is surrounded by dense forests that generate a lot of pollen. "This whole region is a really tough place to live with allergies and asthma," said Curt Chaffin, a Chattanooga physician who specializes in treating asthma patients. "About 70 to 80 percent of the people with asthma have an allergic trigger, and the high pollen counts and climate tend to boost the amount of allergens in the air."[17]

> " Asthma rates are particularly high in places where people live in poverty. Many of those places are found in inner-city neighborhoods where air pollution is thick, cigarette use is heavy, and living conditions are often unclean. "

Asthma and Poverty

Asthma rates are particularly high in places where people live in poverty. Many of those places are found in inner-city neighborhoods where air pollution is thick, cigarette use is heavy, and living conditions are often unclean. According to the Centers for Disease Control and Prevention, 17 percent of children who live in families with incomes below the poverty line have been diagnosed with asthma. Some studies have found the incidence of asthma among poor people even higher—a 2003 study by Harlem Hospital in New York City found that 25 percent of the children who live in Central Harlem, an impoverished, 24-block area of New York City served by the hospital, suffer from asthma.

Sadi Fofana, a 7-year-old boy, lives in a tiny Harlem apartment. The boy's building is old and leaky, which means rainwater enters the walls and promotes the growth of mold. The building is also very dusty and plagued by roaches, rats, and mice. Droppings from those animals include allergens that can aggravate the lungs of asthma patients. Sadi says he suffers terribly in the building. "I would cough so bad, ooh, it feels like I'm going to throw up," he says. "Sometimes, I couldn't breathe so bad I thought I might die."[18]

Moreover, Sadi's parents are immigrants from Mali in western Africa and do not understand English very well. As such, they have misunderstood the directions for administering Sadi's medication, meaning he has often taken it incorrectly and therefore was not receiving the full benefit of his inhaler. Finally, Harlem Hospital assigned a social worker to Sadi's family who worked with his parents to make sure they know how to administer the boy's medicine.

> " **Dust mites consume skin cells shed by humans and live in bedding, upholstered furniture, and carpeting.** "

The social worker also visited the family's apartment, finding heavy coats of dust in the boy's environment. The social worker convinced Sadi's parents to throw out an old rug in the apartment, provided the family with a vacuum cleaner, and donated bunk beds to the family so that Sadi and a young sister, who also has asthma, could sleep a few feet above the floor. The social worker also hired a handyman to patch holes in the walls and an exterminator to get rid of the vermin. Social workers have found similar conditions in other Central Harlem homes. Vincent Hutchinson, a physician at Harlem Hospital who heads the facility's neighborhood asthma intervention program, said hospital officials were surprised by the enormity of the asthma problem in the community served by the medical center. He says, "I'm not sure we understood just how big this was when we decided to do it, but we knew how important it is to intervene at an early age, because asthma is a progressive disease. The earlier you treat it and get it under control, the less severe it gets later on."[19]

Dust Mites, Cockroaches, and Mold

Up close a dust mite resembles a creature out of a science fiction movie—the bulbous, eight-legged beast appears as though it can tear down walls to get to its prey. In reality, dust mites can be seen only through a microscope. (They are arachnids and therefore are related to spiders.) They consume skin cells shed by humans and live in bedding, upholstered furniture, and carpeting. As obnoxious as a dust mite may appear to be, it is the critter's fecal matter that does the real damage—it is an allergen that is particularly irritating to the lungs of asthma patients.

Equally problematic for asthma patients are the droppings from cockroaches, which the insects leave around homes. Also the saliva and other bodily emissions from cockroaches can aggravate the bronchial tubes of asthma patients, often prompting symptoms. While dust mites cannot be seen, cockroaches are certainly large enough to be noticed, but what a lot of people do not understand is that if they see a cockroach in the kitchen and smash it, they have by no means solved their cockroach problem. According to the Asthma and Allergy Foundation of America, if somebody sees a cockroach darting across the kitchen floor, it is safe to assume that another 800 are living elsewhere in the home, usually around sinks, in closets, and other out-of-the-way places.

> " Six-year-old Jahmere Parkinson suffers from asthma, but that did not stop three members of the family from smoking. "

Mold can also trigger asthma. As homes become more energy efficient, there is less circulation of air that can sweep the mold spores from homes. As such, asthma sufferers often see their conditions worsen in energy efficient homes, particularly in winter when windows remain closed.

Tobacco Smoke as a Trigger

Cigarette tobacco includes some 4,000 different chemicals, many of which can aggravate and inflame the bronchial tubes of asthma patients. The damage occurs mainly from inhaling tobacco smoke exhaled by somebody else, better known as secondhand smoke. A study by the Environmental Protection Agency (EPA) concluded that the asthma symptoms of as many as 1 million American children are aggravated by the tobacco smoke exhaled by their parents. Says an EPA report on secondhand smoke and asthma, "Many of the health effects of secondhand smoke, including asthma, are most clearly seen in children because children are most vulnerable to its effects. Most likely, children's developing bodies make them more susceptible to secondhand smoke's effects and, due to their small size, they breathe more rapidly than adults thereby taking in more secondhand smoke."[20]

> " Perhaps the biggest challenge for asthma patients is enduring the American environment—both inside and outside their homes. "

As part of the Harlem Hospital outreach program, a social worker found seven members of the Parkinson family living in a tiny apartment. Six-year-old Jahmere Parkinson suffers from asthma, but that did not stop three members of the family from smoking. After meeting with the social worker, Jahmere's mother said she and the boy's father would try hard not to smoke around Jahmere, but she could not seem to convince Jahmere's grandmother to give up cigarettes in the apartment. "My husband and I usually smoke when the kids aren't around, and we're trying to work out a plan to quit," says Jahmere's mother, Monique Woods-Parkinson. "My mom, that's another matter."[21]

Hay Fever and Pet Dander

About 25 percent of hay fever sufferers eventually develop asthma. (Despite its name, hay fever is not caused by hay, nor does it prompt fever in patients.) Hay fever—officially known as allergic rhinitis—is caused by pollen emitted by weeds, grass, and trees. Since different varieties of plants emit pollen during different times of the year, asthma patients must always be on guard.

Hay fever occurs when the pollen enters the body—either through the nose or eyes. The body's natural immune system attacks the pollen cells, dispatching a chemical known as histamine. The histamine affects nerve endings in the nose and other parts of the respiratory system, causing itching, sneezing, and runny noses.

The result of the histamine's warfare against pollen cells is that elements of the respiratory system, including the bronchial tubes, become inflamed, while the production of mucus to coat the tubes is stepped up. Those are, of course, symptoms of asthma, which is why hay fever can touch off an asthma attack. Somebody who simply suffers from hay fever will sneeze a lot; in an asthmatic person, the symptoms often cause wheezing and shortness of breath. "This type of chronic inflammatory response makes the lung more sensitive to all substances known to precipitate wheezing," adds Phil Lieberman of the University of Tennessee College of Medicine. "Thus an exposure to an allergen can enhance the lung's sensitivity to the other factors known to produce asthma, such as weather conditions, respiratory irritants . . . and exercise."[22]

> Allergies are passed on from generation to generation, meaning that in many people allergies are hard-wired into their DNA—they are born with them, and as they grow older their allergies often develop into asthma.

Those other irritants could also include cat and dog dander. Dander is the tiny flakes of skin that are shed by cats, dogs and other animals. The flakes include microscopic quantities of saliva and urine from the animal. Dander clings to fur but is ultimately kicked off by the animal when it scratches or grooms itself. The dander then comes to a rest on furniture, carpeting, and people's clothes. Dander can also be shed by parakeets and similar pet birds. Whatever its origin, pet dander often triggers asthma symptoms.

Asthma and the Environment

Perhaps the biggest challenge for asthma patients is enduring the American environment—both inside and outside their homes. On the inside, they must be wary of dozens of household products such as paints and cleaners that emit noxious fumes that can irritate their bronchial passages and touch off asthmatic episodes. They must even be careful around gas stoves, which emit nitrous oxide, a chemical that can irritate bronchial passages.

Certainly, asthma patients can take steps on their own to ensure their homes are safe, but when they step outdoors they are at the mercy of their environments. Cities in which air pollution is a daily part of life are particularly hard on asthma patients. Smoggy conditions, often combined with cold temperatures or high humidity, can prompt asthma attacks because of the high content of sulfur dioxide in the air.

Other irritants are ozone and particulate matter—dust, soot, ash and other particles that are suspended in the air after they are emitted from smokestacks or car exhausts. According to the environmental group Natural Resources Defense Council, 159 million Americans—over half the population—live in conditions that could prompt asthma patients to lapse into attacks. Moreover, the council says, about 30 percent of childhood asthma cases can be directly attributed to pollution in the air.

Born with Allergies

Many people can thank their parents or other close relatives for their allergic conditions, although not necessarily their asthma. Researchers have identified 100 genes common in asthma patients, but the research has not yet proved that asthma is passed on from generation to generation, mostly because cases in which children do not inherit the condition from their parents are common.

However, science has established that allergies are passed on from generation to generation, meaning that in many people allergies are hardwired into their DNA—they are born with them, and as they grow older their allergies often develop into asthma. "We do know with certainty that this condition runs in families," says Lieberman. "If one person is allergic, the chance that each child will be allergic is approximately 33 percent. If both parents are allergic, the chance that each child will be allergic is approximately 50 to 70 percent."[23]

Asthma can be triggered by the littlest enemy—the tiny dust mite—or from a product as familiar as a paint can, or from the smog that hangs over many large American cities or even by the family dog. Certainly, many asthma patients can take steps to ensure their homes are friendly to their lungs, but once they step outdoors they are at the mercy of their environments.

Primary Source Quotes*

What Causes Asthma?

66 Heredity plays a major role in the development of asthma, as asthma and allergy often occur in families. . . . Individuals who are susceptible to asthma appear to have inherited specific genes for allergy, asthma, and bronchial hyper-responsiveness. 99

—Francis V. Adams, *The Asthma Sourcebook*. New York: McGraw-Hill, 2007.

Adams is a pulmonary specialist and a professor of clinical medicine at New York University.

66 All I could smell was the exhaust from the cars, a stench that most people didn't even seem to care about. I was sad to have left behind our beautiful farm and all of our animals. I soon started having difficulty breathing whenever I played or exercised. My parents took me to the doctor, who said that I had asthma. 99

—Erica Fernandez, "Playing for Keeps," *Earth Island Journal*, Winter 2008.

Fernandez, 16, started suffering from asthma after moving from a farm in rural Mexico to the city of Oxnard, California.

* Editor's Note: While the definition of a primary source can be narrowly or broadly defined, for the purposes of Compact Research, a primary source consists of: 1) results of original research presented by an organization or researcher; 2) eyewitness accounts of events, personal experience, or work experience; 3) first-person editorials offering pundits' opinions; 4) government officials presenting political plans and/or policies; 5) representatives of organizations presenting testimony or policy.

❝About seven years ago I moved again—this time to New York City. Unfortunately, my symptoms came back. It wasn't just poor air quality that was giving me trouble; it was also allergies. I found that I was especially allergic to cats. They triggered full-on wheezing.❞

—Rich Julason Jr., "Chlorine Triggers My Asthma, but I'm Still a Triathlete," Asthma: Living with Asthma, August 1, 2009. www.health.com.

Julason, 35, who works as a medical devices salesperson, is an asthma patient and a competitor in triathlons.

❝It wasn't until she was 6 years old that an allergist diagnosed [my daughter] with asthma. Tests showed that she was allergic to dust and animal dander, and we found out that cold air also triggered her asthma.❞

—Kelly Harmsen, "As a New Mom, I Struggled with My Daughter's Chronic Cough," Asthma: Living with Asthma, August 1, 2009. www.health.com.

A resident of Chicago, Illinois, Harmsen is the mother of Chrysa, an asthma patient.

❝What is clear is that inner-city patterns (housing, external environment, interaction with medical care, and other factors) place poor, African-American inner-city children at a pronounced risk for asthma, and especially severe asthma.❞

—Cindy Dell Clark, "Breathing Poorly: Childhood Asthma and Poverty," in *Child Poverty in America Today: Health and Medical Care*, ed. Barbara A. Arrighi and David J. Maume. Westport, CT: Greenwood, 2007.

Clark is associate professor of human development and family studies at Pennsylvania State University.

❝Most likely, the disease known as asthma is a spectrum of conditions, and likewise, the causes of asthma are a complex interaction of different factors. A constellation of causes is likely to gradually emerge.❞

—Lara J. Akinbami, "The State of Childhood Asthma, United States, 1850–2005," *Advance Data*, Centers for Disease Control and Prevention, December 12, 2006. www.cdc.gov.

Akinbami is a Washington, D.C., pediatrician who is associated with the Centers for Disease Control and Prevention's Office of Analysis and Epidemiology.

❝Although I was a fairly normal, fun-loving kid, I had one nagging health problem. I had constant bouts with asthma. Every time the leaves fell in Michigan, my asthma would kick up and I had real problems trying to breathe.❞

—Alice Cooper, *Alice Cooper, Golf Monster: A Rock 'n' Roller's Life and 12 Steps to Becoming a Golf Addict.* New York: Three Rivers, 2007.

Cooper, who was born Vincent Damon Furnier, is a rock singer who rose to stardom in the 1970s.

❝Cat allergen can even be found in homes where cats have never been and in office buildings or public places where animals are not allowed. This is because cat allergen is particularly sticky and is carried on clothing from places with cats to other locations. It is almost impossible not to be exposed to some level of cat allergens.❞

—Ellen W. Cutler, *Live Free from Asthma and Allergies.* Berkeley, CA: Ten Speed, 2007.

Cutler is a doctor of chiropractic medicine who practices in Mill Valley, California.

❝I don't have asthma, but my sister Marta does, as do at least 20 other people I know, most of whom take medications to control it. We all live in East Harlem, which has the highest rates of asthma in New York City.❞

—Natalie Olivero, "Asthma, Poverty and Pollution," *Gotham Gazette*, September 2006. www.gothamgazette.com.

Olivero, 17, lives in East Harlem, New York.

Facts and Illustrations

What Causes Asthma?

- Children born by cesarean section suffer asthma at a rate that is **20 percent** higher than other children; it is believed that during their deliveries they are exposed to bacteria that spark asthma symptoms.

- Between **40 and 50 percent** of children who suffer from eczema, a skin rash caused by allergies to household products, animal dander, and other substances, also develop asthma.

- Asthma patients often cover their mattresses and pillows with plastic covers so they will not be exposed to dust mites, but a 2008 study published in the medical journal the *Lancet* concluded that such precautions have no effect on controlling **dust mite infestation**.

- Up to **60 percent** of inner-city asthma patients are sensitive to allergens emitted by cockroaches, according to the Asthma and Allergy Foundation of America.

- According to the Environmental Protection Agency, as many as **300,000** asthma patients under the age of 18 months breathe in **secondhand smoke** exhaled by their parents or other adults.

- Each year, up to **15,000** young asthma patients who breathe secondhand smoke from their parents' cigarettes must be hospitalized.

- A 2008 study found that obese people are likely to suffer from asthma symptoms at a rate nearly **three times higher** than that of other people.

Causes of High Regional Childhood Asthma Uncertain

Many states in the Northeast and some in the Midwest have childhood asthma rates of nearly 10 percent or more of their under-18 populations. Although the triggers of asthma attacks are well known, experts are less certain about the actual causes of asthma. Climate and air quality are often cited as causes but the Centers for Disease Control and Prevention caution that many other factors contribute to high rates of asthma in certain regions of the United States.

4.4–7.8 percent
7.9–8.5 percent
8.6–9.7 percent
Over 9.8 percent
Data not reliable

Source: *Advance Data*, "The State of Childhood Asthma, United States, 1980–2005," Lara J. Akinbami, December 29, 2006. www.cdc.gov.

- About **80 percent** of Hispanics, **65 percent** of African Americans, and **57 percent of whites** live in areas where poor air quality can prompt asthma symptoms, according to the Environmental Protection Agency.

The "Asthma Capitals" of America

Each year, the Asthma and Allergy Foundations of America assesses living conditions for asthma patients in 100 American cities and develops a ranking of the nation's "asthma capitals." In developing the list, the foundation looks at such factors as air quality, poverty rate, and access to smoke-free public places. In 2009, St. Louis, Missouri, was named the nation's worst place for asthma patients. The city with the most favorable conditions for asthma patients was Cape Coral, Florida.

2009 Rank	Metro area	Annual pollen score	Air quality	100% public smoke-free laws	Poverty rate	Uninsured rate	School inhaler access law
1	St. Louis, MO	Worse	Worse	Worse	Better	Average	Average
2	Milwaukee, WI	Average	Worse	Worse	Worse	Better	Average
3	Birmingham, AL	Average	Worse	Worse	Worse	Average	Average
4	Chattanooga, TN	Average	Worse	Worse	Worse	Average	Average
5	Charlotte, NC	Worse	Worse	Worse	Worse	Average	Average
6	Memphis, TN	Average	Worse	Worse	Worse	Average	Average
7	Knoxville, TN	Better	Worse	Worse	Worse	Average	Average
8	McAllen, TX	Worse	Better	Worse	Worse	Worse	Average
9	Atlanta, GA	Average	Worse	Worse	Average	Average	Average
10	Little Rock, AR	Worse	Worse	Worse	Average	Average	Average

● Worse than Average   ◖ Average   ○ Better than Average

Source: Asthma and Allergy Foundation of America, "Detailed Rankings for Metro Areas," January 28, 2009. www.aafa.org.

- A South Korean study found that washing laundry in water heated to 140°F (60°C) **kills all dust mites** in the clothes, and laundry washed in water heated to just 104°F (40°C) kills only **6.5 percent** of dust mites.

People Take Many Steps to Prevent Asthma Attacks

Keeping a cleaner house and reducing exposure to cigarette smoke are the top two steps people take to avoid asthma attack triggers, according to a 2007 survey of adult asthma sufferers and parents of child asthma sufferers. Other steps commonly taken to reduce the chance of asthma attacks include spending less time outdoors and controlling household pets.

Question: To reduce exposure to asthma symptom triggers, which of these, if any, have you done in your home?

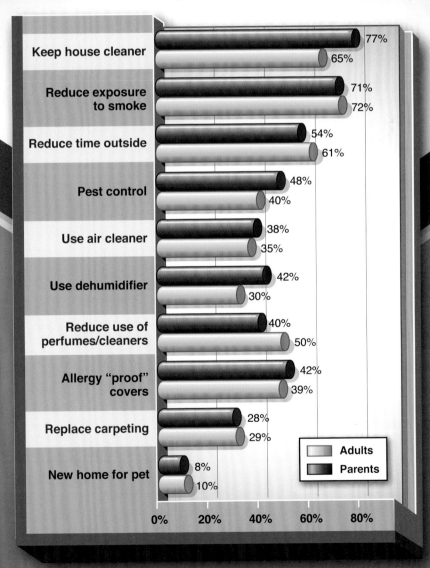

	Parents	Adults
Keep house cleaner	77%	65%
Reduce exposure to smoke	71%	72%
Reduce time outside	54%	61%
Pest control	48%	40%
Use air cleaner	38%	35%
Use dehumidifier	42%	30%
Reduce use of perfumes/cleaners	40%	50%
Allergy "proof" covers	42%	39%
Replace carpeting	28%	29%
New home for pet	8%	10%

Source: HarrisInteractive, *National Consumers League: Asthma Study*, May 15, 2007. www.nclnet.org.

- Because many live in inner-city neighborhoods, **African Americans** are three times more likely than other people to die from asthma.

- **Global warming** may be contributing to an increase in the number of asthma patients. A study by the University of Helsinki in Finland found that higher temperatures prompt stronger winds, which blow pollen over greater distances.

- A 2009 study by Nottingham University in England found that people whose bodies are deficient in **vitamin C** develop asthmatic conditions at a rate **12 percent** higher than people whose vitamin C levels are normal.

- A New York Health Department study found that nearly **14 percent** of adults who were exposed to the **massive dust cloud** raised by the September 11, 2001, destruction of the World Trade Center later exhibited asthma symptoms.

- A study of 880 bakery workers in Germany found **30 percent** exhibiting allergic reactions to wheat flour; moreover, within 3 years of starting their jobs, **7 percent** of the bakery workers experienced asthmatic episodes.

- Babies who reach the age of four months during wintertime are **30 percent** more likely to develop asthma, according to a Vanderbilt University study. The authors of the study speculated that babies often contract respiratory tract infections common during winter, and these infections can lead to asthma.

- Young children who are given acetaminophen, the painkilling ingredient of Tylenol, are **46 percent** more likely to develop asthma symptoms, according to a European study. The drug lowers levels of glutathione, a chemical that protects the lungs against infections.

How Is Asthma Diagnosed and Treated?

66At first I didn't pay too much attention to the wheez-ing in my chest. Gradually, though, it got worse, and my parents took me to see a doctor. The first thing he checked for were allergies, and I did have a lot of allergies. Then, we went to see an allergist who diag-nosed my condition as exercise-induced asthma.**99**

—Tom Dolan, member of the U.S. Olympic swim team and winner of two gold medals.

Beating Asthma in the Pool

Amy Van Dyken was diagnosed with asthma at the age of 18 months. As she grew older she often stayed indoors while her friends played outside, fearful that she would lapse into an asthma attack while jumping rope or playing other games. "One day, when I was 6, I wished out loud that I could be normal and play all the games I saw my friends playing,"[24] Van Dyken says.

Her mother overheard her and took her to see a doctor, who suggested that she take up swimming to build up lung strength. Van Dyken took lessons and joined a local swim team, but during her first race she could not even make it down the length of the pool. She says, "I couldn't swim. I couldn't breathe. I couldn't do anything. That's because I had asthma."[25]

Van Dyken refused to give up. Progress was slow—it took her until the age of 12 before she could swim from one end of the pool to the other. Eventually, she joined her high school swim team, but she often had to drop out of practice and even some races after suffering asthma attacks in the pool.

Meanwhile, Van Dyken followed her doctor's orders very closely, using her inhaler to keep her lungs open. To cope with her asthma, Van Dyken would find herself using three separate medications to keep her bronchial passages open.

> "To cope with her asthma, [Amy] Van Dyken would find herself using three separate medications to keep her bronchial passages open."

Eventually, Van Dyken enjoyed a stellar career as a high school and college swimmer and member of the U.S. Olympic swim team. She competed in the 1996 and 2000 Olympics, winning six gold medals. After winning the first of her gold medals, Van Dyken told an interviewer what it was like standing on the podium and listening to the national anthem played: "It was the best feeling I've had in my whole life. It was especially exciting because of the things I had to overcome with my asthma."[26]

Testing for Asthma

Doctors diagnose asthma by first determining whether patients have family histories of asthma or whether anyone else in the family suffers from allergies to pollen, animal dander, and other common asthma triggers. The patient will also receive a physical examination that focuses on the respiratory tract, looking for congestion in the lungs and nose. Using a stethoscope, the doctor will listen for sounds of wheezing while the patient breathes. Also, the doctor will examine the skin of the patient, looking for rashes and hives because allergies that manifest themselves in skin irritations often trigger asthma as well.

Finally, the patient will perform a spirometry test, which will gauge lung function. To take the test the patient will draw deep breaths and then be asked to exhale forcefully into a hose connected to a device known as a spirometer. The spirometer shows the maximum amount of air the patient can inhale and exhale and the maximum amount of air the patient can exhale in one second.

The physician compares the results against standards for people of similar ages and physical characteristics. Below-normal readings indicate that the airways are obstructed. A healthy person can exhale 80 percent of the air in his or her lungs in the space of a second. People with asthma can typically exhale just 50 percent of the air in their lungs.

Allergy Tests

People who suffer from asthma are often tested for allergies to see what may be triggering their attacks, because once people can identify their triggers, they can take steps to eliminate those substances from their lives. There are a number of ways doctors test for allergies; among the most common are the skin prick, intradermal, skin patch, and blood tests.

In a skin prick test, the doctor will scratch or prick the skin of the patient, then introduce a small amount of the allergen to the test area. The allergen is often an extract that includes pollen, animal dander, or similar substances that may aggravate asthmatic conditions. If a rash develops a few minutes after the skin is pricked, it means the patient's immune system has summoned antibodies to attack the invading substance, and therefore the patient is allergic to that substance. An intradermal test is similar, except the doctor uses a needle to inject the allergen into the skin. (During the test, the needle is not injected all the way through the skin into a blood vessel, but rather between two layers of skin.) In a skin patch the allergen is applied to a patch that is placed over the skin and held tightly against the body's surface by adhesive tape. In time the allergen will seep into the skin, causing a rash if the patient is allergic to the substance in the patch.

> " Using a stethoscope, the doctor will listen for sounds of wheezing while the patient breathes. "

The blood test produces similar results, but in a test tube. During the test a blood sample is withdrawn from the patient, and then different allergens are introduced into the sample. The blood is examined under the microscope for evidence that antibodies have attacked the allergen. If the allergen draws a large number of antibodies, the blood's natural immunity has perceived the allergen as a threat, and therefore it is likely the patient is allergic to that substance.

The Peak Flow Meter

Unlike some other disorders, asthma requires active involvement of patients in treatment. Most asthma patients regularly monitor their lung capacity using a peak flow meter. The meter is a simple handheld device that tests lung strength by measuring how hard the patient can blow air out of his or her lungs.

The meter measures how much air the patient is able to blow out during one fast and hard exhale. The meter makes the measurement in liters of air per minute (although the patient's puff lasts only a couple seconds.) The top score recorded by the meter could be as high as 800 liters per minute, and the bottom score is 0. Meters for children may feature shorter ranges. Doctors want the patient to establish a personal best, which will serve as a baseline—the maximum amount of air the patient can blow out at a time when he or she is not bothered by asthma symptoms.

> **The [peak flow] meter measures how much air the patient is able to blow out during one fast and hard exhale.**

Once the personal best is established, the patient will be asked to use the meter regularly and record the results. If the patient's performances start dropping relative to his or her personal best, the doctor will likely adjust the patient's medication. If the patient records a peak value between 65 and 80 percent of his or her personal best, it is likely the patient is suffering from asthma symptoms. A value below 50 percent of personal best usually indicates a severe asthmatic episode.

Phil Lieberman of the University of Tennessee College of Medicine says peak flow readings serve as an important tool for doctors. In many cases, Lieberman says, patients do not tell the truth about the severity of their asthma attacks—often telling their doctors that their distress during their episodes was not very bad. Once the doctor examines the patient's recent peak flow readings or takes a new one in the office, Lieberman says, the physician can see evidence that the patient's lung capacity is on the decline. "Some patients underestimate their attacks, and in this case a peak flow measurement is essential to prevent serious episodes,"[27] he says.

Inhalers and Nebulizers

Asthma medication is available in injection and pill form, but most asthma patients receive their medication through their inhalers. These are small devices that provide them with a shot of medication right into their bronchial passages, opening up their airways. Inhalers may be used for daily treatments or for emergency use.

Asthma patients with more extreme cases may have to use nebulizers, which are machines that provide a larger dose of the drug through a mist that is inhaled through a tube or mask. Hospital emergency rooms employ nebulizers for asthma patients in respiratory distress, but machines designed for home use are available as well.

> " Physicians are not sure how they work, but they believe corticosteroids affect the patient's DNA, turning off the genes that spark inflammation of the bronchial tubes. "

Whether they use inhalers or nebulizers, asthma patients receive doses of drugs, usually daily or twice daily to keep their bronchial passages open. These are anti-inflammatory drugs, most of which belong to a class of medications known as corticosteroids. Their job is to prevent the bronchial passages from becoming inflamed. Physicians are not sure how they work, but they believe corticosteroids affect the patient's DNA, turning off the genes that spark inflammation of the bronchial tubes. Other commonly used maintenance drugs belong to a class known as bronchodilators; in other words, they open up the bronchial passages. They work by sparking a chemical reaction that relaxes the muscles in the bronchial tubes. Some medications combine corticosteroids with bronchodilators.

Most asthma patients also carry a second inhaler reserved for emergency situations when they feel an attack coming on. Also known as rescue drugs, these emergency medications are bronchodilators formulated to act quickly, opening up the bronchial passages within a few minutes of being inhaled.

Additional Protection

Asthma patients who suffer from specific allergies sometimes take drugs that provide them with protection—such as antihistamines or decongestants that are used to treat hay fever. They may receive injections to improve their immunities against allergens.

Colds and flu can worsen asthma symptoms—viruses that cause the infections can trigger asthma symptoms, particularly since the symptoms of viral infections often include congested airways and a buildup of mucus. Says Van Dyken, "Basically if I get a simple cold, it will usually end up causing problems with my asthma."[28]

> "If asthma patients do come down with colds or flu, doctors advise them to take their peak flow readings often and to seek adjustments in their asthma medications should their symptoms grow worse."

Therefore, asthma patients like Van Dyken are often urged by their doctors to take steps to avoid catching those ailments, such as staying away from others who are contagious, washing their hands often, and avoiding touching their eyes, nose and mouth, which serve as points of entry for cold and flu germs. Also, doctors advise asthma patients to get annual flu vaccinations—for asthma patients, most doctors recommend they take the vaccinations in mist form rather than as injections. If asthma patients do come down with colds or flu, doctors advise them to take their peak flow readings often and to seek adjustments in their asthma medications should their symptoms grow worse.

Alternative Therapies

Many asthma patients have sought alternative therapies that have included herbal concoctions, changes in diet, massive doses of vitamin C, yoga, and acupuncture. Vitamin C is believed to bolster the immune system, helping the patient endure allergies. In yoga, participants learn to control their asthma symptoms through relaxation techniques. In acupuncture, practitioners insert needles into specific parts of the body under the theory that ailments can be controlled by interrupting the transmission of energy that flows from point to point. Doctors are dubious of such methods and urge asthma patients not to give up their inhalers for herbal remedies or similar alternative treatments.

One alternative therapy that many asthma patients try is the Buteyko method, first developed by Russian physician Konstantin Buteyko in the 1950s. Buteyko believed that the lungs of asthma patients are affected during times when the patient is not undergoing distress. He called the condition "hidden hyperventilation," meaning that asthma patients breathe in too much air. Normal lungs breathe in 4 to 6 liters of air per minute, but Buteyko found that asthma patients often breathe in 14 liters per minute.

By practicing the Buteyko method, asthma patients perform exercises that help them inhale less air during their nondistress periods under the theory that with less air inundating the lungs, the bronchial passages will be less inflamed. Patients practice by keeping their mouths closed while breathing, which reduces the amount of air that enters their lungs. Advocates of the Buteyko method caution patients to keep using their inhalers, but many patients who have tried the method say they find themselves relying on their medicine much less. "I've improved quite well," says Penny White, a 51-year-old asthma patient from New Kensington, Pennsylvania, who practices the Buteyko method. "I feel better and I have more control over my asthma."[29]

Others doubt the effectiveness of any treatment that does not include corticosteroids and bronchodilators. "I'm actually very leery of treatments that don't come through your doctor,"[30] says Van Dyken. Indeed, most asthma patients know they must be vigilant in taking their peak flow readings, following their doctor's instructions, and not pushing themselves too hard in their physical fitness programs.

How Is Asthma Diagnosed and Treated?

❝It's important that youngsters diagnosed with asthma learn that it is something that you could control, and not let it control you by stopping you doing what you want to do. Asthma does not stop you from doing sports, in fact sport can help, by making the lungs stronger.❞

—Paula Radcliffe, *Paula: My Story So Far*. Leicestershire, England: Charnwood, 2006.

Radcliffe, an British asthma patient, holds 10 world records in long-distance running.

❝I have to take my bronchodilator inhaler with me everywhere, just in case of emergencies. I have one in the car, one in my desk, one in my purse, and one in my gym bag. I have to use it before I exercise and when I feel an asthma attack coming on.❞

—Laura Finlayson, "My Chronic Cough Turned Out to Be Adult Asthma," Asthma: Living with Asthma, August 1, 2009. www.health.com.

Finlayson is a 38-year-old asthma patient who lives in Westwood, New Jersey.

* Editor's Note: While the definition of a primary source can be narrowly or broadly defined, for the purposes of Compact Research, a primary source consists of: 1) results of original research presented by an organization or researcher; 2) eyewitness accounts of events, personal experience, or work experience; 3) first-person editorials offering pundits' opinions; 4) government officials presenting political plans and/or policies; 5) representatives of organizations presenting testimony or policy.

66When the kids were young, we spent a lot of time showing them how to use their inhalers and making sure they did it right. I don't have asthma, but I practiced with an inhaler anyway so that I could help them learn. It's amazingly easy to do it wrong and have the medicine land at the back of your throat or on the roof of your mouth instead of your lungs.99

—Denise Grady, "Learning to Live with Asthma," *Good Housekeeping*, August 2007.

Grady is the mother of two sons, both of whom are asthma patients.

66Over the past 70 years I have seen very little change in the treatments available for people like me with chronic asthma. The packaging and delivery systems are different, but the medications are essentially the same. I am still waiting for the wonders of modern science to allow me to be asthma free.99

—Elayne Lofchie, "Living with Asthma: Our Stories," American Asthma Foundation, 2009. http://americanasthmafoundation.org.

Lofchie has suffered from asthma since the age of 13.

66Eczema, hay fever and a family history of asthma . . . are often associated with asthma but they are not necessarily elements of an asthma diagnosis. There is no single satisfactory diagnostic test for all asthma.99

—Anna Murphy, *Asthma in Focus*. London: Pharmaceutical Press, 2007.

Murphy is a respiratory pharmacist at University Hospitals in Leicester, England.

66 In many individuals the failure to use a peak flow meter despite severe asthma is one indicator of who may suffer a fatal attack. . . . Many patients do not accept that they have asthma and that it is a chronic disease that requires regular monitoring and medication. **99**

—Francis V. Adams, *The Asthma Sourcebook*. New York: McGraw-Hill, 2007.

Adams is a pulmonary specialist and a professor of clinical medicine at New York University.

66 Experts in the field of asthma have suggested that Buteyko breathing exercises can improve asthma symptoms in some people, and there is some research to support this belief. However, it is important to recognize that it does not provide a cure for asthma but, used alongside conventional asthma treatment, it may help some people to cope better with their symptoms. **99**

—Rob Hicks, *Beat Your Allergies: Simple, Effective Ways to Stop Sneezing and Scratching*. London: Penguin, 2007.

Hicks is a London, England–based physician and author.

66 Some asthmatics believe that taking a lot of medications will help cure them. But asthmatics should understand that medications only treat symptoms, they do not cure asthma. **99**

—Ellen W. Cutler, *Live Free from Asthma and Allergies*. Berkeley, CA: Ten Speed, 2007.

Cutler is a doctor of chiropractic medicine who practices in Mill Valley, California.

How Is Asthma Diagnosed and Treated?

- Asthma patients spend more than **$6 billion** a year on prescription drugs.

- A study of 540 Canadian asthma patients found that **a third of them were misdiagnosed** with asthma and that they exhibited no symptoms after they stopped using their inhalers. Authors of the study found that in many cases, physicians had not employed **spirometry tests** in making their diagnoses.

- When asthma patient Tom Dolan won a gold medal in men's swimming at the 1996 Olympics, doctors found that his lungs were inhaling just **10 percent** of the oxygen that healthy lungs would inhale.

- A British study found that **peak flow meters** often give inaccurate readings of lung capacity. The study examined four meters used by 12 children, and found all four failed to detect at least two-thirds of asthmatic episodes among the patients.

- In 2007 physicians in Taiwan tested the effectiveness of **acupuncture** on 16 asthma patients and found the technique improved their symptoms by **10 percent**; however, the physicians concluded that bronchodilating drugs are more effective than acupuncture.

- A side effect of corticosteroid use is osteoporosis, a condition that results in **brittle bones**. A Malaysian study found that some asthma patients who use corticosteroid drugs start showing symptoms of osteoporosis within six months of commencing their use.

Asthma Patients Prefer Self-Management over Doctor Visits

Most asthma patients would rather adjust their own medications than consult with a doctor when symptoms become bothersome, according to the results of a study published in 2006. The study provides a glimpse into the attitudes of asthma patients toward their medications and the adjustments that they make as their conditions worsen or improve.

Attitude statement	Agree
I want to take treatments that provide immediate relief	90%
I am confident I know my asthma well enough to intervene early to try and prevent worsening conditions	85%
I use my medication as and when necessary	82%
I am much more likely to try to manage my asthma myself, rather than visit my physician as soon as my symptoms become bothersome	71%
I prefer to adjust my medication to the changes of my asthma, taking less when feeling well and more when feeling worse	68%
I am concerned about taking higher doses of medication due to possible side effects	59%
I am concerned about taking too much medication when I am well	54%
Despite taking my medication as my doctor tells me to, I still have a fear of having a serious asthma attack	49%
When I feel well, I believe there is no need to take my medication every day	39%
I would prefer to take a high dose of medication to try to avoid as many symptoms as possible	35%

Source: Martyn R. Partridge et al., "Attitudes and Actions of Asthma Patients on Regular Maintenance Therapy: The INSPIRE Study," *BMC Pulmonary Medicine*, June 13, 2006. www.biomedcentral.com.

Asthma Attacks Sometimes Require Hospitalization

Hospitalization is sometimes the only way to ensure appropriate treatment of an asthma attack. Length of stays vary, depending on the severity of the attack and, often, the age of the patient. A Kansas study found that the average length of a hospital stay for an asthma patient in the state is 3 days. Younger patients—those under the age of 15—recover much more quickly than older patients and can be released after shorter hospital stays.

Average Length of Stay for Asthma Hospitalizations by Age Group (2003–2007)

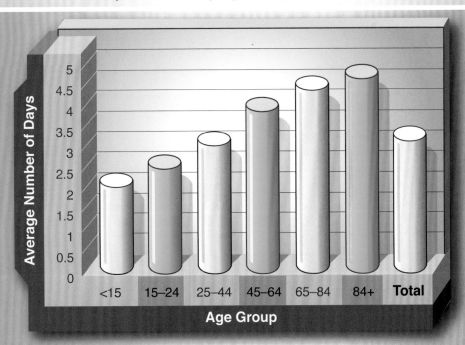

Source: Kansas Department of Health and Environment, *Kansas Asthma Burden Report 2009*, April 2009. www.kdheks.gov.

- A study published in the *Journal of Allergy and Clinical Immunology* found that as many as a third of asthma patients skip their bronchodilator doses because of the drugs' side effects, which include **nervousness and jitteriness**.

Lack of Money or Insurance Affects Patients' Medication Decisions

One-third of adult asthma patients surveyed as part of a 2007 study said they take less than the prescribed dose of medication because they cannot afford more or because their insurance does not cover it. Adult patients also take less or parents give their children less than prescribed doses of medication when asthma attacks are not severe.

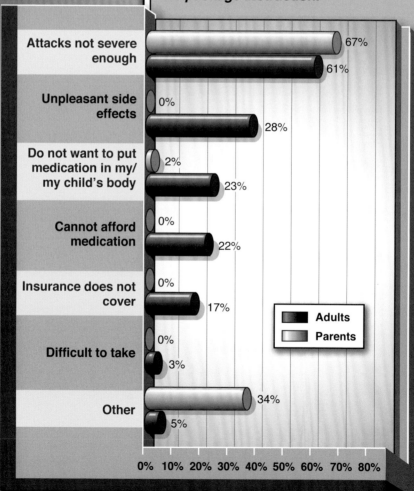

Question: Please indicate which of the following are reasons why you take/ your child takes less of the fast-acting (or rescue) inhaler than indicated on the package instruction.

Reason	Adults	Parents
Attacks not severe enough	61%	67%
Unpleasant side effects	28%	0%
Do not want to put medication in my/my child's body	23%	2%
Cannot afford medication	22%	0%
Insurance does not cover	17%	0%
Difficult to take	3%	0%
Other	5%	34%

Source: HarrisInteractive, *National Consumers League: Asthma Study*, May 15, 2007. www.nclnet.org.

- A Syracuse University study of 20 asthma patients enrolled in a yoga class found that their symptoms eased by an average of **43 percent** after practicing **yoga** over a period of 10 weeks.

- Russian physician Konstantin Buteyko concluded that asthma patients draw in **14 liters** of air per minute when they are not suffering from symptoms; a normal person draws in **between 4 and 6 liters** of air per minute.

- A study reported in the *London Daily Mail* found that the **Buteyko method helped ease symptoms** in nearly all 600 patients who participated in the study and that **98 percent** of the patients found themselves using their inhalers less often.

- About 400 people worldwide have undergone a new treatment for asthma that uses **heat to kill muscles** in the bronchial passages; when the muscles die they are unable to constrict and reduce air flow to the lungs.

- Healthy people can exhale **80 percent** of the air in their lungs in the space of a second; asthma patients can typically exhale just **50 percent** of the air in their lungs in a second.

- A patient who blows out a value below **50 percent** of his or her personal best on a peak flow meter is likely to be undergoing an asthma attack.

How Do People Live with Asthma?

"I have learned to live with my asthma. All my friends know about it and are very supportive. I hope that when I'm older, my asthma will go away. But if it doesn't, I'll be just fine."

—Brooke Frost, 11, of Oceanside, New York.

Achieving Good Control

Asthma patients seek what is known as "good control"—the ability to manage their symptoms. This is usually accomplished by finding the right medication as well as recognizing the triggers that can lead to asthma attacks. Once they achieve good control, asthma patients should be able to maintain a normal lifestyle. "[Asthma] is not that big a deal," says Micah Jarrett, an asthma patient and college baseball player from Salisbury, North Carolina. "It won't limit you from doing the things you want to do. I'm still able to go out and play baseball, but I have to be a little smarter about it."[31]

Jarrett says that to maintain good control, he keeps an eye on his symptoms. If he finds himself out of breath while playing ball, he must ask himself whether he is simply tired or whether his lungs are warning him that an asthma attack is imminent. "Asthma is serious and you've got to take it seriously,"[32] he says.

Asthma patients maintain good control over their conditions if their symptoms are limited to twice a week or less and they have no need for emergency medications. Also, they are controlling their conditions if they maintain good lung function while performing normal activities, their sleep is normal, their peak flows stay above 80 percent of their personal best numbers, and they suffer from no more than a single asthma attack per year.

Many doctors urge their asthma patients to become active participants in their own care—to take their medications on schedule, to learn to recognize their symptoms, and to be able to identify their asthma triggers. "For an asthma treatment strategy to succeed, the patient must be an active participant," says Francis V. Adams of New York University. "Patients who participate in their own care are better educated in regard to their illness and can communicate well with their physicians. These characteristics are extremely important in managing bronchial asthma."[33]

Making a Home Asthma Friendly

Homeowners can take many steps to make a home asthma friendly. According to the Environmental Protection Agency (EPA), the first step people can take to make their homes less irritating to asthma patients is not to smoke—or at the very least, not to permit smoking indoors.

As for what can be done from room to room, in the bedrooms the EPA urges families of asthma patients to use plastic covers over pillows and mattresses, which will help keep dust mites from finding homes in bedding. Also, the EPA recommends washing sheets and blankets once a week in hot water.

In addition, the agency recommends homeowners dust their homes often with damp cloths and to vacuum carpets and fabric-covered furniture. Since cockroaches are attracted to food and garbage, the EPA recommends that all food be kept in sealed containers and not left exposed in the kitchen, and that garbage cans be emptied regularly. As for spraying pesticides to control insects, the EPA warns that some pesticides could trigger allergic reactions, so if people use them they should make sure there is good ventilation in the room and that asthma patients stay out of the sprayed area for several hours after the pesticides are used.

> " Asthma patients maintain good control over their conditions if their symptoms are limited to twice a week or less and they have no need for emergency medications. "

Mold forms due to dampness, so the EPA urges homeowners to take steps to eliminate sources of moisture—contractors may have to be called in to fix roofs as well as walls and other places where moisture may be leaking into a home. Carpets may become moldy after they are exposed to moisture, so these may have to be replaced. Also, mold often forms on the walls of kitchens and bathrooms, so the EPA recommends that people open windows while cooking or showering and use exhaust fans as well.

Asthma Friendly Products

In 2008 the Asthma and Allergy Foundation of America (AAFA) began a program to certify household products as "asthma and allergy friendly." Among the products that have received that designation are bedding and mattresses, toys, flooring, and paint. The foundation also rates vacuum cleaners and washing machines for their abilities to remove allergens from clothing and carpets.

One substance the certification program looks for in household products is the chemical di(2-ethylhexyl)phthalate, also known as DEHP. The chemical is commonly used in household drainpipes and in wallpaper, flooring, furniture, shower curtains, clothes, raincoats, shoes, and toys. DEHP is known to trigger asthma symptoms. Moreover, products tend to give off minute particles of DEHP, meaning they are often inhaled by asthma patients.

Finding stuffed animals that are asthma friendly is particularly challenging, since stuffed animals act as sponges for dust and other allergens. Some manufacturers have found ways to make stuffed animals asthma friendly mostly by not using dyes that could spark allergic reactions. Still, even the manufacturers of the toys acknowledge that the products have to be washed regularly to keep them asthma friendly. One manufacturer of a stuffed bear that has received AAFA certification recommends the toy be placed in a freezer bag

> " The EPA urges families of asthma patients to use plastic covers over pillows and mattresses, which will help keep dust mites from finding homes in bedding. "

and frozen for 24 hours, then machine washed. Moreover, the freezing and washing process should be repeated every four weeks. And since the toys go through a monthly freezing and washing cycle, they must be made out of resilient fabrics that can stand up under that degree of wear and tear.

Finding Hypoallergenic Pets

Soon after the family of President Barack Obama moved into the White House in early 2009, a story that made constant headlines concerned the president's pledge to his two daughters on the night he won the election—that Sasha and Malia Obama had earned the puppy that would be joining the Obamas in the White House.

Since Malia Obama has asthma, the Obamas were forced to look for a hypoallergenic dog, meaning a dog whose dander would be less likely to trigger Malia's asthma symptoms. After a search that spanned several months, the Obamas selected a Portuguese water dog, a breed that is known to shed less dander than other breeds. The dog, which they named Bo, has short hair and does not shed a lot of its hair, which is what spreads the allergens around the home.

> " Since Malia Obama has asthma, the Obamas were forced to look for a hypoallergenic dog, meaning a dog whose dander would be less likely to trigger Malia's asthma symptoms. "

Other dogs considered to be hypoallergenic are the bichon frise, Irish terrier, Chihuahua, and various poodles. Dogs that shed a lot of hair and are therefore best avoided by asthma patients include cocker spaniels, Irish setters, dachshunds, basset hounds, German shepherds, and Afghan hounds.

Asthma patients are less likely to find hypoallergenic cats. Even cats with short hair can spark asthmatic symptoms because the allergens are transmitted in the cat's saliva, which the animal uses to groom its fur. Therefore, as the cat rolls around on the carpet or sleeps on its favorite chair, the animal is leaving its allergens around the house.

Exercising and Asthma

Many athletes are able to compete at high levels even though they suffer from asthma. Usually, asthma patients function better in sports that feature short bursts of activity followed by periods of rest, such as baseball, tennis, sprinting, and volleyball. Soccer, basketball, hockey, and long-distance running are endurance sports and are not considered to be ideal for asthma patients.

Swimming in chlorinated water can trigger an asthma attack, but some asthma patients find ways to compete in aquatic sports. As a ninth-grade student, Linda Dunklee of Garden City, Michigan, tried out for her school's swim team even though she is asthmatic. "I suffered through week after week, attack after attack, too proud to quit but too tired to continue," Dunklee recalled. "There were too many people to let down and too many expectations to live up to for me to give up."[34]

Dunklee found her best event was the backstroke because it enabled her to draw air into her lungs for virtually the entire race. Still, racing was a challenge. Dunklee's teammates supported her, urging her to continue even as she neared the point of exhaustion, then helping her out of the pool at the end of the race or practice.

> **Although asthma cannot be cured, it may be possible to outgrow the condition, meaning some asthma patients simply stop experiencing symptoms.**

All of Dunklee's dedication paid off. In the first race of her sophomore year, Dunklee entered the 100-yard (91.4m) backstroke. She swam hard during the race, fighting against the pain in her chest as her lungs struggled to draw in air. When the race ended, Dunklee touched the wall and stood in her lane. "I was very confused," she said. "No one else was at the wall. I heard cheers from my teammates and saw the jaw-dropped look on my coach's face. I spun around to see five girls still swimming."[35]

Dunklee had beaten everybody to the wall, winning the race by an astounding margin of seven seconds. She has since become one of the stars of her team. "Every day I struggle, every length I gasp, every turn I ask myself why," she says. "But when I see improved times, when I win races, and when I take four medals at a league meet no one expected me even to qualify for, I know the struggle was worth it."[36]

Outgrowing Asthma

Although asthma cannot be cured, it may be possible to outgrow the condition, meaning some asthma patients simply stop experiencing symptoms. A 2005 Colorado study found that 6 percent of asthma patients stop experiencing symptoms by the age of 18. Doctors are not sure why; they suggest some patients' bodies may mature and be better able to handle the stresses of allergens and other irritants.

The same study found that a much larger number of patients—39 percent—have less-severe symptoms by the age of 18. Still, those statistics indicate that the vast majority of asthma patients will carry their condition from childhood into adulthood. "The numbers show that most do not [outgrow asthma]," says Andrew Ting, a pediatric pulmonologist at Mount Sinai Medical Center in Boston, Massachusetts. "That's why we're hesitant to tell parents [their children] are going to outgrow it."[37]

And even those patients who have outgrown their asthma may see it return. A New Zealand study found that a third of patients who can be regarded as asthma free by the age of 18 will see a return of symptoms by their late twenties. "The results suggest that once one has asthma there is no guarantee that the person can be rid of it,"[38] says Robin R. Taylor, the University of Otago physician who headed the study.

Making Lifestyle Changes

While their symptoms may ease as they grow older, it is likely that people who develop asthma as children will be burdened with their condition for the rest of their lives. To maintain good control and therefore live normal lives, asthma patients know they have to be constantly vigilant and on the watch for the allergens and other substances that trigger their symptoms.

That is by no means a simple task. As asthma patients enter their adult years, they may find themselves living busy lives and being responsible for a lot more than just making sure their carpets stay clean. Kenya Shelton was among those adults whose asthma symptoms seemed to disappear as she left childhood. As an adult she became a busy professional working as a business administrator while teaching school at night and keeping up an active social life. Then one Saturday night she started wheezing and coughing. Friends saw that Shelton was unable to catch her breath and called an ambulance. She was rushed to a nearby hospital.

The emergency room doctors saved her life. Shelton spent seven days in the hospital. After returning home, she has paid a lot more attention to the environment around her. Shelton reads food labels, searching for allergens that she knows will trigger an asthmatic episode. She takes her asthma medication religiously, avoids restaurants and other places where people smoke, and exercises regularly. "I have accepted the fact that I have a chronic disease," says Shelton. "I am asthmatic, but it took a frightening experience for me to fully come to terms with my illness."[39]

> She takes her asthma medication religiously, avoids restaurants and other places where people smoke, and exercises regularly.

Shelton's experience illustrates that asthma patients may be able to find places to live that are asthma friendly. They may be able to compete in sports and live with hypoallergenic dogs. As children they may be able to cuddle stuffed animals. Deep inside their lungs, though, their bronchial tubes can constrict and grow inflamed at any moment, meaning that asthma patients must always be aware that when it comes to breathing, there are no guarantees.

Primary Source Quotes*

How Do People Live with Asthma?

66 I swam every chance I had, working not only on lung capacity but stroke mechanics, turns, starts, and muscle-building. When I couldn't get to a pool, I ran until my lungs burst and my legs burned. 99

—Linda Dunklee, "Fast Lane," *Teen Ink*, January 2009.

Dunklee is an asthma patient and a member of her high school swim team in Garden City, Michigan.

66 I know some people who have asthma so bad that they have to carry their inhaler with them to go running. Mine doesn't seem to be that bad, and my symptoms come and go in fits. 99

—Rich Julason Jr., "Chlorine Triggers My Asthma, but I'm Still a Triathlete," Asthma: Living with Asthma, August 1, 2009. www.health.com.

Julason, 35, who works as a medical devices salesperson, is an asthma patient and a competitor in triathlons.

* Editor's Note: While the definition of a primary source can be narrowly or broadly defined, for the purposes of Compact Research, a primary source consists of: 1) results of original research presented by an organization or researcher; 2) eyewitness accounts of events, personal experience, or work experience; 3) first-person editorials offering pundits' opinions; 4) government officials presenting political plans and/or policies; 5) representatives of organizations presenting testimony or policy.

Primary Source Quotes

66Unfortunately, eliminating asthma and allergy triggers isn't as easy as buying an air filter or a mattress cover, although both these measures can help. You'll never completely get rid of all allergens, especially dust mites.**99**

—Mayo Clinic, "Asthma Friendly Products: Do They Help Reduce Symptoms?" November 19, 2008. www.mayoclinic.com.

Based in Rochester, Minnesota, the Mayo Clinic is one of the top research and training hospitals in America.

66A hypoallergenic cat is one that is not as likely to cause an allergic reaction in humans who were previously allergic to cats. Although there is no scientific proof, the Siberian and Russian Blue cat breeds are said to be naturally hypoallergenic.**99**

—Felines4us.com, "Hypoallergenic Cats," 2008. www.hypoallergeniccats.org.

Felines4us.com is an online service that matches prospective cat owners with breeders and other owners who wish to place cats in new homes.

66If you have asthma and you are sensitive to certain animals, your asthma is likely to be worse if they live in your home. Having pets to which you are allergic is not a good idea.**99**

—Mark Levy, Trisha Weller, and Sean Hilton, *Asthma at Your Fingertips*. London: Class, 2006.

Levy is a physician who practices in Middlesex, England; Weller is a respiratory nurse; and Hilton is a professor at St. George's University of London.

66 If symptoms don't have a significant and negative impact on their lifestyle, many patients don't pay too much attention to the disease and don't treat it properly. This puts them at greater risk for having severe and even fatal asthma attacks. **99**

—Courtney Crim, "Asthma Facts from Dr. Crim," 2009. www.asthma.com.

Crim is a Chapel Hill, North Carolina, pulmonary disease physician.

66 Asthma control is possible for most people who have asthma. That means you can expect to live an active life without being bothered by daily or nightly asthma symptoms. The catch is that you generally will need to be on a long-term controller medication to achieve that. **99**

—Kathi MacNaughton, "Is Less Asthma Medication in Your Future?" MyAsthmaCentral.com, May 21, 2007. www.healthcentral.com.

MacNaughton, an asthma patient who lives in Boise, Idaho, contributes commentaries about asthma to MyAsthmaCentral.com.

66 Brian still has occasional attacks and can't afford to ignore respiratory infections, even ones that seem minor. He had a bout with pneumonia his freshman year in college and needed an inhaler for the first time in years. That illness was a sobering reminder to all of us that although asthma loosened its grip over time, it never did let go entirely. **99**

—Denise Grady, "Learning to Live with Asthma," *Good Housekeeping*, August 2007.

Grady is the mother of two sons, both of whom are asthma patients.

Facts and Illustrations

How Do People Live with Asthma?

- Every day in America, **40,000** people miss school or work due to asthma.

- The *New England Journal of Medicine* reports that children who spend their preschool years in day care centers are less prone to develop asthma because they are able **to build up resistances** to infections that can trigger asthma symptoms.

- According to the American College of Sports Medicine, athletes who suffer from **exercise-induced asthma** can usually avoid symptoms if they perform **warm-up exercises** 45 to 60 minutes before their competitions or practices. The rest period between the warm-up and the activity enables lungs to recover.

- The American Academy of Allergy, Asthma and Immunology reports that **25 percent** of American homes have levels of dust mite infestation in bedding high enough to trigger asthma symptoms.

- A study of 600 children in Costa Rica found an asthma rate of **28 percent** among patients whose bodies are deficient in **vitamin D**. Asthma patients can enhance their levels of vitamin D by consuming fortified dairy products and orange juice or by regularly spending time in sunlight.

- A study that examined the medical records of more than 8,000 people found those with high levels of **folic acid** in their bodies are better able to fight off the symptoms triggered by allergens. Folic acid is a component of leafy green vegetables such as spinach and kale and of green peas, wheat germ, and avocados.

Reducing Allergens at Home Can Help Asthma Sufferers

People spend a third of their lives in their bedrooms, so controlling allergens in a bedroom can make life easier for people with asthma. A few simple steps can help control common indoor allergens such as those created by dust and pets.

Bed and bedding. Encase pillows, mattresses, and box springs in dust mite–proof covers. Wash sheets, pillowcases, and blankets at least once a week in water heated to at least 130° F.

Curtains and blinds. Washable curtains made of plain cotton or synthetic fabric. Replace horizontal blinds with washable roller-type shades.

Windows. Close windows and rely on air conditioning during pollen season. Clean mold and condensation from window frames and sills.

Air filtration. Choose an air filter that has a small-particle or HEPA filter.

Furnishings. Choose easy-to-clean chairs, dressers, and nightstands made of leather, wood, metal, or plastic. Avoid upholstered furniture.

Clutter. Remove items that collect dust.

Pets. Keep pets out of the bedroom. Bathing pets at least twice a week may reduce the amount of allergen in the dander they shed.

Flooring. Remove carpeting and use hardwood or linoleum flooring, or washable area rugs. Or use low-pile instead of high-pile carpeting and vacuum weekly with a vacuum cleaner that has a high-efficiency particulate air filter. Shampoo the carpet frequently.

Source: Mayo Clinic, "Allergy-Proof Your House," April 8, 2009. www.mayoclinic.com.

77

Many Asthma Patients Fail to Get Their Prescriptions Filled

Researchers in Michigan studied the habits of 1,064 asthma patients to see how well they were complying with their doctors' orders and found a high number do not get their corticosteroid inhaler prescriptions filled. Level of adherence was judged on a scale of 0 to 100, 0 being never filling prescriptions and 100 being always filling them. Looking at the group as a whole, researchers found that more than half filled their prescriptions less than 50 percent of the time. The researchers also broke down the results by race, concluding that African Americans and other groups are less likely to get their prescriptions filled than whites. Asthma patients who do not get their prescriptions filled risk not having their inhalers available in the event of an asthma attack.

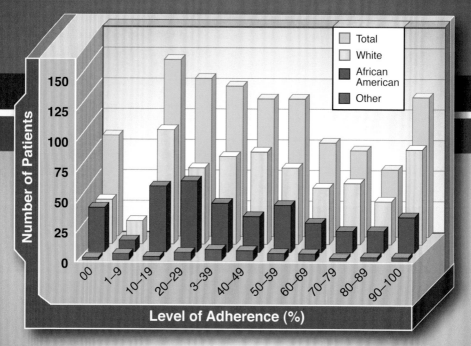

Source: L. Keoki Williams et al., "Patients with Asthma Who Do Not Fill Their Inhaled Corticosteroids: A Study of Primary Nonadherence," *Journal of Allergy and Clinical Immunology*, November 2007. www.jacionline.org.

- A British study found that wheezing declines in asthma patients who drink a glass of **apple juice** every day. Natural chemicals in the juice known as **flavonoids** appear to have a calming effect on the muscles of the bronchial tubes.

Adults Are More Limited by Asthma than Children

Adults are more likely to limit their activities because of asthma than are children, according to a 2007 survey of adults with asthma and parents of children with asthma. The activity that adults limit most is participation in sports. However, the survey also shows that in all instances, less than half of adults (and in many cases less than a fourth) actually limit their activities because of asthma.

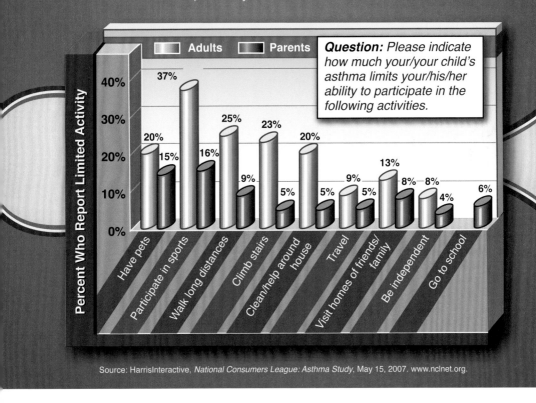

Source: HarrisInteractive, *National Consumers League: Asthma Study*, May 15, 2007. www.nclnet.org.

- The medical journal *Annals of Allergy, Asthma and Immunology* reported the results of a study that found asthma patients **over the age of 65** saw their doctors less often and made fewer trips to emergency rooms than younger patients. The study said older patients are more scrupulous in the use of their inhalers than are younger asthma patients.

Key People and Advocacy Groups

Asthma and Allergy Foundation of America: The foundation sponsors a program to identify allergy-friendly products such as bedding, mattresses, flooring, paint, and toys. Also, washing machines and vacuum cleaners are assessed for their abilities to remove allergens from clothing and carpets. Ratings for consumer products can be found at the foundation's Web site at www.asthmaandallergyfriendly.com. The foundation also issues an annual list of the top 10 "asthma capitals" in America, meaning the places where asthma patients suffer the most due to climate, pollution, and lack of no-smoking laws.

Jerome Bettis, Jackie Joyner-Kersee, Amy Van Dyken, and Tom Dolan: Bettis is a former professional football player, and Joyner-Kersee, Van Dyken, and Dolan are Olympic medalists. All are asthma patients. They have served as important role models for young people who suffer from asthma, proving that it is possible to live a normal life with asthma and excel in sports.

Konstantin Buteyko: The Russian physician (who died in 2003) developed a breathing method for asthma patients. The Buteyko method teaches patients to draw less air into their lungs during nonstress periods. The technique has helped to reduce bronchial inflammation in many asthma patients, who believe they can get by with less medication while practicing the Buteyko breathing method.

Harlem Hospital: The impoverished Central Harlem neighborhood of New York City has some of the highest asthma rates in the county—25 percent of the community's children suffer from asthma. Harlem Hospital has established an outreach program, sending social workers into the neighborhood to ensure that young asthma patients know how to use their inhalers and that their families learn about ways to create more asthma-friendly homes.

Hippocrates and Galen: Hippocrates, a Greek who lived in the fourth century B.C., was among the first physicians to describe the symptoms of asthma accurately. Galen, a Greek physician who lived about 400 years later, linked the condition to a blockage in the bronchial tubes.

Kathi MacNaughton: An asthma patient who lives in Boise, Idaho, MacNaughton has written dozens of commentaries and essays about asthma that are available at the MyAsthmaCentral.com Web site. In addition to her commentaries, MacNaughton reports news about developments in asthma treatments.

Moses Maimonides: The twelfth-century Middle Eastern physician was the first to notice that asthma symptoms grow worse during the rainy season—probably due to mold spores that accompany damp conditions. He urged asthma patients to seek refuge in the desert, thus becoming the first doctor to recommend that asthma patients avoid the allergens that trigger their symptoms.

Natural Resources Defense Council: Based in New York City, the environmental group has sponsored research into a number of environmental issues, including the impact of air pollution on asthma patients. The organization's Web site, www.nrdc.org, contains a number of resources on asthma, including the effects of fumes from diesel school buses on asthmatic school students as well as air quality found in American schools.

Malia Obama: The daughter of President Barack Obama and First Lady Michelle Obama is an asthma patient. Malia's condition drew national attention to the plight of asthma patients as the Obamas spent months searching for a hypoallergenic dog for the White House. The Obamas finally selected a Portuguese water dog, a short-haired breed known to shed less dander than other breeds.

Chronology

1940s
Isoprenaline, one of the first bronchodilators, is used to treat asthma patients.

Fourth century B.C.
Greek physician Hippocrates first describes the symptoms of asthma.

1600s
Italian physician Bernardino Ramazzini links asthma to dust.

1100s
Moses Maimonides, court physician to the Middle Eastern emperor Saladin, urges asthma patients bothered by mold spores to seek refuge in the desert.

1900s
Many doctors adopt the notion that asthma is a mental illness and begin treating asthma patients for depression.

1100   1500   1600   1850   1900   1950

First century B.C.
Galen, a Greek physician, links asthma to blockages in the bronchial passages.

1864
British doctor Hyde Salter finds that animal dander triggers asthma. Salter also recommends that the herb belladonna, which has anti-inflammatory properties, could be used as an asthma drug.

1500s
Belgian physician Jan Baptista van Helmont suggests asthma is a disease of the lungs.

1950
Cortisone, an anti-inflammatory drug, is first used as a treatment for asthma. Cortisone will later be developed into the class of anti-inflammatory drugs known as corticosteroids.

1950s
Russian physician Konstantin Buteyko develops a breathing method that helps reduce the inflammation in the bronchial tubes of asthma patients.

2007
Scientists in Australia identify a gene they believe is responsible for causing asthma. The discovery provides the strongest evidence to date that children inherit asthma from their parents or other close relatives.

1998
A study by the University of Iowa finds that asthma afflicted 22 percent of the American athletes who competed at that year's Winter Olympics.

1950

2000

2010

1960s
Anti-inflammatory drugs go into widespread use to treat asthma.

2003
Harlem Hospital reports that some 25 percent of children who live in Central Harlem are afflicted with asthma, a finding that further connects asthma with poverty.

2008
In Beijing, China, government officials order factories closed and cars to remain off the streets for several days before the Olympic Games begin. Officials feared that air pollution would prompt symptoms in asthmatic athletes and others who have trouble breathing.

2009
The Obamas move into the White House and begin the search for a hypoallergenic dog that will not aggravate the asthma symptoms of daughter Malia. A Portuguese water dog named Bo is selected.

Related Organizations

American Academy of Allergy, Asthma and Immunology (AAAAI)

555 E. Wells St., Suite 1100

Milwaukee, WI 53202-3823

phone: (414) 272-6071

e-mail: info@aaaai.org • Web site: www.aaaai.org

The AAAAI is the professional organization representing physicians who treat asthma patients as well as others whose allergies trigger symptoms. Visitors to the organization's Web page can learn how to avoid allergens, how young asthma patients who leave for college can manage their symptoms, and how to recognize allergens in food.

American Asthma Foundation (AAF)

4 Embarcadero Center, Suite 3150

San Francisco, CA 94111

e-mail: info@americanasthma.org

Web site: http://americanasthmafoundation.org

The AAF provides grants to physicians and scientists pursuing research into asthma. The foundation also serves as an advocacy group for asthma patients. Students can find personal stories of asthma patients on the foundation's Web site.

American Kennel Club (AKC)

8051 Arco Corporate Dr., Suite 100

Raleigh, NC 27617-3390

phone: (919) 233-9767

Web site: www.akc.org

The organization that represents dog breeders has made resources about how to select a hypoallergenic dog available on its Web site. The AKC lists 11 breeds that it says are less likely than other dogs to spark asthma symptoms.

American Lung Association (ALA)

1301 Pennsylvania Ave. NW, Suite 800

Washington, DC 20004

phone: (212) 315-8700

Web site: www.lungusa.org

The ALA serves as an advocate for patients who suffer from a number of pulmonary diseases, including asthma. By visiting the organization's Web site, asthma patients can learn about the disease as well as its treatment options. Also, employees concerned with the safety of their workplaces can find a number of resources on occupational asthma.

American Medical Association (AMA)

515 N. State St.

Chicago, IL 60610

phone: (800) 621-8335

Web site: www.ama-assn.org

The national association representing American physicians has provided its members with direction for treating asthma. Students can find many resources on the association's Web site about asthma, including the AMA's 2009 *Report of the Council of Scientific Affairs*, which defines the condition, provides an overview of treatment options, and discusses environmental factors that trigger symptoms in patients.

Centers for Disease Control and Prevention (CDC)

Office of Communication

Building 16, D-42

1600 Clifton Rd. NE

Atlanta, GA 30333

phone: (800) 311-3435

e-mail: cdcinfo@cdc.gov • Web site: www.cdc.gov

The federal government's chief public health agency explores trends in diseases and other conditions that affect the health of Americans. Visitors to the CDC's Web site can find many statistics about asthma, such as emergency room admissions and mortality rates. The CDC's pamphlet *You Can Control Your Asthma—a Guide to Understanding Asthma and Its Triggers* can be downloaded through the Web site.

Environmental Protection Agency (EPA)

Ariel Rios Building, 1200 Pennsylvania Ave. NW

Washington, DC 20460

phone: (202) 272-0167

Web site: www.epa.gov

The EPA enforces federal laws that ensure protection of the environment. Students can find many resources about asthma on the EPA's Web site, including information on ozone, secondhand smoke, mold, and controlling cockroaches and dust mites.

National Institutes of Health (NIH)

9000 Rockville Pike

Bethesda, MD 20892

phone: (301) 496-4000

e-mail: nihinfo@od.nih.gov • Web site: www.nih.gov

The NIH is the chief funding arm of the federal government for medical research. Many resources about asthma are available on the agency's Web site, including reports of NIH-sponsored studies into ozone and dust mites as well as information on gas stoves, air pollution, and the genetic characteristics of asthma.

Occupational Safety and Health Administration (OSHA)

200 Constitution Ave. NW

Washington, DC 20210

phone: (800) 321-6742

Web site: www.osha.gov

An agency of the U.S. Labor Department, OSHA ensures that American companies follow laws written to protect workers. By visiting the OSHA Web site, students and workers can find the federal laws written to protect workers from breathing fumes or particles that could lead to occupational asthma. The Web site also lists the rights of workers and recommends steps they can take if they suspect the air in their workplace is unsafe.

World Health Organization (WHO)

Avenue Appia 20

1211 Geneva 27

Switzerland

phone: +41 22 791 2111 • fax: +41 22 791 3111

e-mail: info@who.int • Web site: www.who.int/en

WHO is the public health arm of the United Nations. Visitors to the WHO Web site can find many resources on asthma's impact on people who live in developing nations, where many live in unsanitary conditions that help trigger asthma symptoms. Among the WHO's programs is the Global Alliance Against Chronic Respiratory Diseases, in which member nations sponsor programs to improve the respiratory health of people in developing countries.

For Further Research

Books

Francis V. Adams, *The Asthma Sourcebook*. New York: McGraw Hill, 2007.

Jerome Bettis, *The Bus: My Life in and out of a Helmet*. New York: Doubleday, 2007.

Matthew J. Colloff, *Dust Mites*. Victoria, Australia: CSIRO, 2009.

Ellen W. Cutler, *Live Free from Asthma and Allergies*. Berkeley, CA: Ten Speed, 2007.

Rob Hicks, *Beat Your Allergies: Simple, Effective Ways to Stop Sneezing and Scratching*. London: Penguin, 2007.

Patrick McKeown, *Asthma-Free Naturally: Everything You Need to Know to Take Control of Your Asthma*. San Francisco: Conari, 2008.

Anna Murphy, *Asthma in Focus*. London: Pharmaceutical Press, 2007.

Periodicals

Sarah Brewer, "Breathe Easy—and Control Your Asthma," *London Daily Mail*, March 8, 2009.

Kathleen Doheny, "Obesity Worsens Asthma," *U.S. News & World Report*, September 5, 2008.

Tom Dolan, "Unstoppable," *Guideposts*, July 2004.

Linda Dunklee, "Fast Lane," *Teen Ink*, January 2009.

Erica Fernandez, "Playing for Keeps," *Earth Island Journal*, Winter 2008.

Beth Gollob, "Asthma Sufferers Wonder When They'll Be Able to Breathe Easier," *Oklahoma City Daily Oklahoman*, July 15, 2007.

Denise Grady, "Learning to Live with Asthma," *Good Housekeeping*, August 2007.

Marcus Hayes, "Every Breath Is Precious for Eagles Wide Receiver Hank Baskett," *Philadelphia Daily News*, September 27, 2008.

Jet, "Sweet Victory: Jackie Joyner-Kersee Triumphs over Lifelong Asthma," March 8, 2004.

Laura Flynn McCarthy, "Could It Be Asthma?" *Parenting*, May 2009.

Chris McDaniel, "Not-a-Choo Campers Face Asthma with New Weapons," *Yuma (AZ) Sun*, March 22, 2009.

Marti Parham, "Asthmatic Athletes Urge Sufferers to Take Control of the Disease and Their Lives," *Jet*, May 26, 2008.

Kate Whyman, "Taping It—Good Wheeze," *Times of London*, April 28, 2007.

Internet Sources

Breathe Easy Play Hard Foundation, "Faces of Asthma," 2009. www.breatheeasyplayhard.com/pg/jsp/general/faces.jsp?faces=1.

Environmental Protection Agency, "Secondhand Smoke," January 29, 2009. www.epa.gov/asthma/shs.html.

Harvard University School of Medicine, "Living with Asthma," April 2008. http://hms.harvard.edu/public/disease/asthma/index.html.

Mayo Clinic, "Asthma," May 31, 2008. www.mayoclinic.com/health/asthma/DS00021.

Medical News Today, "All About Asthma," 2009. www.medicalnews today.com/info/asthma/what-is-asthma.php.

Source Notes

Overview

1. Phil Lieberman, *Understanding Asthma*. Jackson: University Press of Mississippi, 1999, p. 3.
2. Lieberman, *Understanding Asthma*, p. 7.
3. Quoted in Lynn Sweet, "In Oregon, Obama Asked, 'How Do I Know I Can Trust You?'" *Chicago Sun-Times*, May 17, 2008. http://blogs.suntimes.com.
4. Quoted in BBC News, "Boys Grow Out of Child Asthma," August15, 2008. http://news.bbc.co.uk.
5. Quoted in BBC News, "Boys Grow Out of Child Asthma."
6. Quoted in Michelle Meadows, "Breathing Better," *FDA Consumer*, March/April 2003, p. 20.
7. Quoted in Robert Fitzgerald, trans., *The Iliad*. New York: Oxford University Press, 1998, p. 375.
8. Francis V. Adams, *The Asthma Sourcebook*. New York: McGraw Hill, 2007, p. 207.
9. Quoted in *Jet*, "Sweet Victory: Jackie Joyner-Kersee Triumphs over Lifelong Asthma," March 8, 2004, p. 22.

What Is Asthma?

10. Lieberman, *Understanding Asthma*, p. 11.
11. Lieberman, *Understanding Asthma*, p. 11.
12. Quoted in Meadows, "Breathing Better," p. 20.
13. Jerome Bettis, *The Bus: My Life in and out of a Helmet*. New York: Doubleday, 2007, p. 26.
14. Quoted in Deanna Martin, "Breathing Room," *Scholastic News*, April 22, 2002, p. 4.

15. Quoted in Geoffrey Cowley and Anne Underwood, "Why Ebonie Can't Breathe," *Newsweek*, May 26, 1997, p. 58.

What Causes Asthma?

16. Quoted in Blythe Bernhard, "St. Louis Is Worst Place to Live for People with Asthma," *St. Louis Post-Dispatch*, January 28, 2009. www.stltoday.com.
17. Quoted in Dave Flessner, "Chattanooga Among Worst for Asthma," *Chattanooga Times Free Press*, January 31, 2009. www.timesfreepress.com.
18. Quoted in Richard Perez-Peña, "Childhood Asthma Project Reaches Out in Harlem," *New York Times*, May 1, 2003, p. B-1.
19. Quoted in Perez-Peña, "Childhood Asthma Project Reaches Out in Harlem," p. B-1.
20. Environmental Protection Agency, "Secondhand Smoke," January 29, 2009. www.epa.gov.
21. Quoted in Perez-Peña, "Childhood Asthma Project Reaches Out in Harlem," p. B-1.
22. Lieberman, *Understanding Asthma*, p. 30.
23. Lieberman, *Understanding Asthma*, p. 33.

How Is Asthma Diagnosed and Treated?

24. Quoted in Mike Gosman, "Swimmers with Attitude," *Swimming World*, August 1996, p. 35.
25. Amy Van Dyken, "Beating the Odds," *Junior Scholastic*, September 4, 2000, p. 10.
26. Quoted in CNN, "Olympic Swimmer Amy Van Dyken on Managing

Asthma," October 27, 1999. www.cnn.com.

27. Lieberman, *Understanding Asthma*, p. 78.

28. Quoted in CNN, "Olympic Swimmer Amy Van Dyken on Managing Asthma."

29. Quoted in J. Michael Krivyanski, "Better Breathing for Asthmatics," *Pittsburgh Post-Gazette*, April 3, 2001, p. F-1.

30. CNN, "Olympic Swimmer Amy Van Dyken on Managing Asthma."

How Do People Live with Asthma?

31. Quoted in Katie Scarvey, "Attacking Asthma," *Salisbury (NC) Post*, August 23, 2009. www.salisburypost.com.

32. Quoted in Scarvey, "Attacking Asthma."

33. Adams, *The Asthma Sourcebook*, p. 117.

34. Quoted in Gerri Hunt, "Cuddle with Confidence: Asthma-Friendly Toys Debut," Kids Today, September 1, 2005. www.kidstodayonline.com.

35. Linda Dunklee, "Fast Lane," *Teen Ink*, January 2009, p. 6.

36. Dunklee, "Fast Lane," p. 6.

37. Quoted in Malika Marshall, "Research Shows Some Children May Outgrow Asthma," WBZ, August 20, 2009. http://wbztv.com.

38. Quoted in Peggy Peck, "Study Raises Doubt About 'Outgrowing' Asthma," Medscape Medical News, May 21, 2003. www.medscape.com.

39. Kenya Shelton, "Second Wind," *Essence*, May 1992, p. 48.

List of Illustrations

Index

Index

About the Author

Hal Marcovitz, a writer based in Chalfont, Pennsylvania, has written more than 140 books for young readers. His other titles in the Compact Research series include *Painkillers*, *Religious Fundamentalism*, *Bipolar Disorders*, *Phobias*, *Hepatitis*, and *Meningitis*.